Dynamic Dialogue

Letting Your Story Speak

Dynamic Dialogue: Letting Your Story Speak
First Edition
Copyright © 2014 William Bernhardt Writing
Programs
Red Sneaker Press
An imprint of Babylon Books

ISBN: 9780989378949

Dynamic Dialogue

Letting Your Story Speak

William Bernhardt

The Red Sneaker Writer Series

Other Books by William Bernhardt

Red Sneaker Writer Series

Story Structure: The Key to Successful Fiction
Creating Character: Bringing Your Story to Life
Perfecting Plot: Charting the Hero's Journey
The Fundamentals of Fiction (DVD)

The Ben Kincaid Series

Primary Justice
Blind Justice
Deadly Justice
Perfect Justice
Cruel Justice
Naked Justice
Extreme Justice
Dark Justice
Silent Justice

Murder One
Criminal Intent
Hate Crime
Death Row
Capitol Murder
Capitol Threat
Capitol Conspiracy
Capitol Offense
Capitol Betrayal

Other Novels

Nemesis: The Final Case of
Eliot Ness
The Code of Buddyhood
Paladins of the Abyss
Dark Eye
Shine

The Midnight Before
Christmas
Final Round
Double Jeopardy
Strip Search

Poetry

The White Bird

For Young Readers

Equal Justice: The Courage of Ada Lois Sipuel (biography)
Princess Alice and the Dreadful Dragon (illus. by Kerry McGhee)
The Black Sentry

Edited by William Bernhardt

Legal Briefs
Natural Suspect

Dedicated to all the Red Sneaker Writers:
You can't fail unless you quit.

"The world requires me to rewrite its wretched dialogue!"

Richard Greenberg

TABLE OF CONTENTS

INTRODUCTION

Welcome to the Red Sneaker Writers series. If you've read other Red Sneaker publications or attended Red Sneaker events, you can skip to Chapter One. If you're new, let me take a moment to explain.

I've been telling stories for many years, doing almost every kind of writing imaginable. I've been speaking at workshops and conferences almost as long. Every time I step behind the podium I see the same tableau staring back at me: long rows of talented people, most of whom have attended many of these events but are still frustrated by the fact that they haven't sold any books. Yes, the market is tough and agents are hard to find and self-publishing can be frustrating. But when aspiring writers do the work, put it out there, but still don't succeed...there's usually a reason. Too often enormous potential is lost due to a lack of fundamental knowledge. Sometimes a little guidance is all that stands between an unknown writer and a satisfying writing career.

I do my best to help at conferences, but the large auditorium/general information lecture is not terribly conducive to writing instruction. And sometimes the teaching I've heard offered is dubious at best. Too often speakers seemed more interested in appearing "literary" than in providing useful information. Sometimes I felt presenters did more to obfuscate the subject than to explain it, that they wanted to make writing as mysterious and incomprehensible as possible, either because that made them sound deeper or because they didn't understand the subject themselves. How is that going to help anyone?

After giving this some thought, I formulated the Red Sneaker Writing Center. Why Red Sneakers? Because I love my red sneakers. They're practical, flexible, sturdy—and bursting with style and flair. In other words, exactly what I think writing instruction should be. Practical, flexible, resilient, useful, but still designed to unleash the creative spirit, to give the imagination a platform for creating wondrous work.

I held the first Red Sneaker Writers conference in 2005. I invited the best speakers I knew, not only people who had published many books but people who could teach. Then I launched my small-group seminars—five intensive days with a handful of aspiring writers. This gave me the opportunity to read, edit, and work one-on-one with people so I could target their needs and make sure they got what would help them most. This approach worked extremely well and I'm proud to say a substantial number of writers have graduated from my seminars and placed work with major publishers. But I realized not everyone could attend my seminars. How could I help those people?

This book, and the other books in this series, are designed to provide assistance to writers regardless of their location. The books are short, inexpensive, and targeted to specific areas where a writer might want help.

Let me see if I can anticipate your questions:

Why are these books so short? Because I've expunged the unnecessary and the unhelpful. I've pared it down to the essential information, practical and useful ideas that can improve the quality of your writing. Too many instructional books are padded with excerpts and repetition to fill word counts required by book contracts. That's not the Red Sneaker way.

Why are you writing so many different books instead of one big book? I encourage writers to commit to writing every day and to maintain a consistent writing schedule. You can read the Red Sneaker books without losing much writing time. In fact, each can be read in a single afternoon. Take one day off from your writing. Read and make notes in the margins. See if that doesn't trigger ideas for improving your work.

I bet it will. And the next day, you can get back to your work.

You reference other books as examples, but you rarely quote excerpts from books (other than yours). Why? Two reasons. First, I'm trying to keep these books brief. I will cite a book as an example, and if you want to look up a particular passage, it's easy enough to do. You don't need me to cut and paste it for you. Second, if I quote from materials currently under copyright protection, I have to pay a fee, which means I'd need to raise the price of the books. I don't want to do that. I think you can grasp my points without reading copyrighted excerpts. Too often, in my opinion, excessive excerpting in writing books is done to pad the page count.

Why does each chapter end with exercises? The exercises are a completely integrated and essential part of this book, designed to simulate part of what happens in my small-group seminars. Samuel Johnson was correct when he wrote: *Scribendo disces scribere.* Meaning: You learn to write by writing. I can gab on and on, but these principles won't be concretized in your brain until you put them into practice.

So get the full benefit from this book. Take the time to complete the exercises. If you were in my seminar, this would be your homework. I won't be hovering over your shoulder when you read this book—but you should do the exercises anyway.

What else does the Red Sneaker Writers Center do?

I send out a free e-newsletter filled with writing advice, market analysis, and other items of interest. If you would like to be added to the mailing list, then please visit: http://www.williambernhardt.com/writing_instruction/index.php. We hold an annual writing conference with a specific focus: providing the information you need to succeed. I lead small-group seminars every summer. The newsletter will provide dates and information about these programs. And there will be future books in this series.

You may also be interested in my DVD set, *The Fundamentals of Fiction*, available at Amazon or on my website. It's about five hours of me talking about writing. Who doesn't want that?

Okay, enough of this warm-up act. Read this book. Then write your story. Follow your dreams. Never give up.

William Bernhardt

CHAPTER 1: DEFINING DIALOGUE

"[A]lways get to the dialogue as soon as possible....Nothing puts the reader off more than a big slab of prose at the start."

P. G. Wodehouse

First let's talk about what dialogue is and isn't. Then we'll talk about what it can do for you.

Dialogue is your friend. Dialogue will improve the pacing and readability of your book. Dialogue will make an otherwise ordinary story sparkle. But it has to be handled correctly. Fortunately, as a Red Sneaker Writer, you aren't content to simply put words down on paper. You want to do it right.

What Is Dialogue?

In my book on Creating Character, I encouraged readers to think of their characters not as real people but as metaphors. Similarly, I'm going to urge you to get away from the often-taught but completely inaccurate idea that dialogue should mirror real-life conversation. Dean Koontz, who is in a position to know, wrote: "Many writers think—erroneously—that fiction should be a mirror of reality. Actually, it should act as a sifter to refine reality until only the essence is before the reader. *This is nowhere more evident than in fictional dialogue."*

Koontz is so right. Fiction readers are not looking for more reality. If they were, they'd read a newspaper, not a novel. Chances are they'd like to get away from reality, so they turn to fiction. Because fiction is so much better.

When Edgar Allan Poe formulated the essential elements of the short story, he mentioned verisimilitude. He did not say a word about reality. Few readers would accuse Poe's work of having excessive reality. But the stories must seem credible, that is, realistic within the world they inhabit. This is necessary to trigger the reader's suspension of disbelief. You make the situation seem plausible enough that the reader is willing to enter your world. And once you have them there, you can have some fun. You can make them laugh or cry. You can provide a feeling of enlightenment or redemption or epiphany too often missing from real life.

So when you create dialogue, remember first and foremost that you are not trying to recreate real life. You want your dialogue to have verisimilitude. That does not mean you should try to duplicate the way people actually talk. You are an artist, not a tape recorder. If you've ever recorded and transcribed actual conversation, you know how awkward, poorly phrased, and banal it can be. You don't want that in your book.

For the most part, I eliminate conversational or performative stutters—"well," "uh," "er," "hmm," and the like. Do people utter these non-words? Of course. Do I want to read it? No. At least not without a good reason. I have on occasion used "Well" at the start of a sentence to show hesitation (Ben Kincaid) or to strike a casual tone or to set up a joke. For the most part, though, what is common in life is tedious on the page. Similarly, I would avoid the grammatical intrusions you often hear—"like" (unless you're writing a Valley Girl character), "really," "kinda," "sorta," "I mean," and their ilk. This is not the stuff of scintillating dialogue.

Contractions are fine. In fact, if you're writing modern-day characters and they don't use contractions, they're likely to come off sounding stiff and robotic. Fragments can work in dialogue, if they reflect the personality of the character, as can run-on sentences (Anne of Green Gables comes to mind). But don't overdo it. The stories readers love most typically feature clever dialogue, snappy patter, and memorable turns of phrases. These don't turn up so much in real life because people don't have time to come up with them. But you do. You can fill your book with all those clever comebacks most people only think of the next day.

Dialogue is not conversation—but it should sound conversational.

Do I Need Dialogue?

Yes, if you're writing fiction, you almost certainly want dialogue. There are books that have survived without dialogue. There are also novels that have survived entirely on dialogue (McDonald's *Fletch* series, for one). Guess which is more popular? Part of this has to do with the way dialogue propels the plot forward. And part of it has to do with eye candy.

P.G. Wodehouse may have been one of the first to note the importance of eye appeal in reading. Books with lots of white space at the margins—created by short paragraphs and dialogue—look friendlier. Long blocky paragraphs of narrative or description or exposition look imminently skippable. Rapid-fire back-and-forth dialogue will make your book more appealing even before your reader has read a word.

You don't believe me? Go to your local bricks-and-mortar bookstore (if there still is one), find a comfortable chair, and watch people shop. It's an enlightening experience. They walk slowly down the aisle, often having no idea what they want to read next. Something catches their eye—a title, some engaging cover art, or the author's name (that's why it's usually at the top). They take the book. They open it up. And in most cases, five seconds later, they put it back on the shelf.

What happened? The potential purchaser may not even have consciously thought about this decision. But something instinctively made them decide that the book did not look like an engaging reading experience. And more often than not, that instinctive reaction comes down to eye appeal. A book with short paragraphs and lots of dialogue looks like it's going to be more fun to read. Few readers are looking for a hair-shirt experience. You have to draw them in.

Dialogue draws readers in. Dialogue makes your story seem immediate, fast-paced, and fun.

Dialogue is a Many-Splendored Thing

Dialogue is incredibly useful because it can accomplish so many different goals. Here's a short list of the many possible purposes:

Revealing characterization. Every aspiring writer hears the catchphrase, "Show, don't tell." (If you don't know what I'm talking about, read my book on Character).

The basic idea is that it's more effective to provide information about emotional states or inner thoughts by indicating it rather than expressly identifying it. Dialogue can be used to reveal motives, or to give insight into character, without overt telling. That's good. Because when you tell, it sounds like an intrusive omniscient narrator is directly feeding information to the reader. ("Sally was depressed.") On the other hand, if Sally is having lunch and talking to her best friend about her feelings, it sounds less intrusive and more natural. ("Madge, I don't know what's wrong with me these days," Sally said. "I can barely drag myself out of bed in the morning.")

See the difference? Both examples give the reader essentially the same information. But the first seems clumsy and amateurish and will have little impact on the reader, while the other directly engages readers' imaginations and makes them want to know more.

Setting the Mood. Similarly, you should avoid overt mood-setting sentences, i.e., "It was a dark and stormy night." It works better if you can do it in a clever or memorable manner, like George Orwell did. "That day all the clocks struck thirteen." But it may be better yet if you can do it in dialogue. How many books or films have a character say something like, "This doesn't feel right..." The dialogue informs the reader that something is not as it should be, which probably means something bad is about to happen. Or, "It's quiet. Too quiet." The naive reader might think quiet is not such a bad thing. Until you tell them otherwise, by having your character describe it in a manner that suggests ominous foreboding. Every good book needs sustained tension, from the first page to the last. Dialogue helps you strike that tone and maintain it.

Intensifying the Conflict. You can always magnify conflict by depicting dramatic, jaw-dropping, earth-shattering, protagonist-devastating events. But a confrontational conversation between adversaries can also ramp up the tension, or remind readers of everything that's at stake. A conversation between protagonist and sidekick could have the same effect. Remember that in the greatest film ever made, *Star Trek II: The Wrath of Khan*, Kirk and Khan never actually meet. But thanks to the magic of 23rd-century viewscreens, they sure do talk to each other a lot.

Ramping Up the Pace. Tension and pacing go hand-in-hand. No matter how well you define the conflict or raise the stakes, the tension will dissipate if the pace lags. Popular fiction generally requires a quicker pace and more external action than other fictional forms, but every novel must maintain its forward momentum. If the reader stops wondering (or caring) what will happen next, the reader is likely to put the book down, never to return.

Good dialogue moves the story forward in an immediate and engaging way. The pages seem to fly by when characters are talking. I think one of the reasons courtroom scenes are so compelling is that they have major conflict and high stakes—but they're basically all dialogue—people talking in a forum where words really matter.

Dialogue can be a useful tool when you have information you must provide to the reader but don't want to grind the story to a halt. At times critical bits of information, background, backstory, or description must be conveyed. In those instances, consider providing the information to the reader in dialogue. If you can concoct a natural way for one character to speak the information to another, it may not impact the pacing. Personally, I would much rather hear a character tell a confidante about their childhood than endure a flashback or flashforward. And I'd rather have a hero tell a sidekick to note some important feature in the environment than put up with a long descriptive passage.

Adding Substance to the Setting. Setting and Description are such tricky subjects that I've decided to devote an entire future book to them. They are necessary to your story, but mishandled, they can be lethal to the pace. You can ease this potential sleeping pill on paper with the skillful use of dialogue. And you don't necessarily have to be obvious about it, as in, Shaggy remarking to Scooby how "creeeeeeepy" this old haunted mansion is.

Part of bringing any environment to life, after all, is observing the people in it and recreating how they talk and how they act. Agents and editors often advise writers not to open a book with description. And yet, if you don't establish setting, the reader will feel hopelessly adrift. Dialogue might help you provide readers with the information that need about the fictional world they've entered without grinding the story to a stop.

Suggesting Theme. Theme is a tricky business, and once again, a topic of such import that it will be the subject of a future book. The trick is to give your story that all-important additional layer, the sense that this story is about something beyond the story itself, that the reader has not only been entertained but enlightened—without letting the reader think you've become dogmatic. No one likes being preached at, and nothing will turn a reader off faster then feeling that the writer has an agenda.

Much better if your character makes a gentle, perhaps even subtle remark that points the reader in the right direction—but trusts them to get there themselves. My novel *Death Row* concerns a convicted murderer about to be executed, so you won't be shocked to hear that part of my thematic goal was to have readers seriously consider the death penalty and whether an erratic, race-skewered judicial system should be taking lives. But no one says that. There is a moment, though, at the celebration party after Ben Kincaid has obtained the release of a death row inmate and the man sees how affectionately Christina acts toward Ben (who is typically oblivious). The man says, "Ben, life is precious. You can't waste a single second." An understandable sentiment from a man who spent years on death row for a crime he didn't commit. But I suspect most of my readers read an additional message into that line of dialogue.

There are undoubtedly other good uses for dialogue, but these are the main ones. Now that you've seen how important dialogue is and how useful it can be, let's discuss how to do it well.

DYNAMIC DIALOGUE

Highlights

1) Dialogue is not conversation—but it should sound conversational.

2) Dialogue is critical to engaging, well-paced fiction.

3) Dialogue can help reveal characterization and motive, set the mood or tone, intensify the conflict, speed up the pace, establish setting, or suggest theme.

Red Sneaker Exercises

1) Look at your outline (read my book on Structure if you haven't got one yet) and identify difficult scenes, particularly the ones that require exposition or backstory. Can some of that information be provided in dialogue? How can you make it sound more like two regular people talking and less like an intrusive author is feeding information directly to the reader?

2) Look at the scenes you've written. Although all books are different, a good rule of thumb is that each chapter in a modern novel should be about fifty percent dialogue (less for action sequences, more for courtrooms or other verbal-confrontation scenes). Can you replace some of those long prose paragraphs with some snappy dialogue?

3) Try recording a casual conversation and transcribing it. You'll likely be amazed at all the conversational stutters, circular constructions, pointless remarks, and unnecessary words. Now rewrite the script to make it better. Remember

what you've learned from this exercise, and when you write your next dialogue passage, restrict yourself to the parts that are worth reading.

CHAPTER 2: DIALOGUE FUNDAMENTALS

"In real life, conversation is often roundabout, filled with general commentary and polite rituals. In fiction, the characters must always get right to the point when they talk."

Dean Koontz

Writing instruction typically does not lend itself to broad proclamations about rules. This is an art, after all, as well as a craft, and both refuse to be chained down. For any rule I proclaim, I know there's a smart English major out there who can identify an instance when an author broke the rule and still produced a fine book. So to paraphrase a famous pirate, I don't offer rules. More like guidelines.

This is nowhere truer than when we discuss dialogue. But here's a principle that comes as close to a rule as anything in writing is ever likely to be:

The best dialogue propels the story forward.

Achieving Forward Momentum

Dialogue needs to be functional, that is, it needs to accomplish one of the many goals mentioned in the previous chapter, plus it needs to be entertaining.

Somnambulant readers do not recommend your work to their friends.

This is yet one more reason why dialogue should not mirror real-life conversation. The truth is, we spend a lot of time messing around instead of communicating with one another. Some of that is the observation of social niceties, such as calling people "ma'am" and "sir" or exchanging meaningless platitudes ("Pleased to meet you."). Some of that is the human tendency to beat around the bush, especially when we're discussing sensitive or personal matters. And some, it must be said, stems from our tendency to, at times, chatter on even when we have nothing to say.

None of that works in fiction. The ho-hum chatter that fills too much of real life is unacceptable. Your dialogue, much like your plot, must seem as if it has a point and a direction. If your readers feel the dialogue is meandering or superfluous, they will start skimming. Sometimes readers skip description to get back to dialogue. If they start skipping your dialogue, there may be nothing left to read— except someone else's book.

When you write dialogue, you must be ruthless. If it isn't essential to your story, if it doesn't fulfill a fundamental purpose, if it doesn't advance the story—cut it out.

Consider this scintillating passage:

> "Hi, my name is Joe."
> Sally stuck out her hand. "Hi, Joe. I'm Sally."
> "Hi, Sally," Joe said, shaking her hand.
> "Pleased to meet you," Sally said.
> "Same here," said Joe.
> "It's an honor."

12

"For me as well."
"Do you live around here?"
"A couple of miles away. On Main Street."
"Oh yes. I have a friend who lives there."
"So do I!"

There are a dozen different things wrong with this passage and we will discuss all of them. But the most critical problem is the fact that the passage gives the reader no useful information about the story or characters. Is it realistic? Sadly, all too realistic. But we read novels to see the mundane transformed into the splendid—not the other way around. In my books, this entire passage would be cut, or perhaps reduced to a passing, "They greeted each other." Then I would plunge into the dialogue that matters. Forget stuff like "How are you?" Instead, lead with: "Did you kill the ambassador?" or perhaps "Who was that bimbo I saw you with last night?"

More Fundamentals

Now that I've explained that there are no rules in writing, let me give you three more:
Good dialogue is compressed and economic.
This principle may be self-explanatory. I don't think there's any place for windy, self-indulgent prose, but it certainly isn't in dialogue. Dialogue is where your writing should snap, crackle, and pop. There shouldn't be any messing about. If you're using dialogue for exposition, get to the point. If you're providing character information or establishing the tone of a relationship, then do it already.

Kurt Vonnegut once said that when he revised his work, he went through his manuscripts word-by-word,

13

asking himself, Must this word be in here? Not can it be. *Must* it be. If it performed no useful or unique purpose, he took it out. This led to some highly readable prose, including some positively riveting and hilarious dialogue. Economy was the hallmark of Vonnegut's style and it worked beautifully for him.

If dialogue is to fulfill its function of accelerating the plot, it must stay lean and mean. You may even have to kill your darlings, if it makes the dialogue maintain that all-important riveting pace.

Good dialogue must have direction and purpose.

If your dialogue is going to move your story forward, then it must seem to have direction, that is, it must seem to be going somewhere—and the reader should never be in doubt about where it is going. The detective in a mystery doesn't mosey about having idle conversations with random people. He interviews suspects. He collects information. Whether the information obtained turns out to be useful or a complete red herring, these conversations move the story forward. The reader understands why these questions are being asked.

At times, the reader may be fooled. The clever writer may hide clues by disguising information as being offered for one purpose, when it actually plants seeds for surprises to come. The conversation still has purpose, even if the reader initially does not grasp all the ramifications of the information provided.

Dialogue should not call attention to itself.

There are a few fundamental things that every person on earth, male or female, young or old, wants. Everyone wants security (which is a complete illusion, sorry, don't kill the messenger). Everyone wants to look good. Everyone wants to be loved. And everyone wants people to think they're smart. Even people who will aggressively tell you they're not smart. No one wants the world to think they're a dummy. Least of all writers.

So it will perhaps not shock you when I tell you that writers have been known on occasion to write clever or poetic prose that attracts attention—for all the wrong reasons (and not just in dialogue). Perhaps you've heard the phrase: You have to kill your darlings? This is what they're talking about. If you've got a bit of dialogue that jumps off the page screaming, Oh, what a clever bit of dialogue am I!—then it has to go. Later, after the reader has finished your magnificent work, they can think about the author who wrote it for them. But while they're reading, you want them immersed in the story, thinking about the fascinating characters and the breathtaking plot—not you.

Now, if you have a clever character that could credibly deliver a witty bon mot, fine. Perhaps you even have a poetic character that could offer a lovely alliterative line or a spellbinding metaphor. But if not, if you're just doing it because you're so proud or it, or because you want everyone to know what a FABULOUS WRITER you are— cut it. Dialogue is where you draw attention to your characters, not yourself.

Highlights

1) The best dialogue propels the story forward.

2) Good dialogue is compressed and economic.

3) Good dialogue must have direction and purpose.

4) Dialogue should not call attention to itself.

Red Sneaker Exercises

1) Look at a dialogue scene you've written. Could you shorten it without losing any essential information? Give it a try. There may be some introductory chatter at the beginning that could be lost, or perhaps some summarizing or departing words. Now reread the scene as edited. Is it better? Faster paced? More engaging?

2) Before you write your next dialogue scene, think about the purpose of the dialogue. Yes, you know the purpose of the scene—but why are you doing it in dialogue? Which of the fundamental purposes of dialogue will this exchange fulfill? Once you've focused on your purpose, you may find it easier to write the dialogue in an engaging and economic fashion.

3) In my book on Story Structure, I discuss how to write scenes rather than sequels, that is, how to focus on the part that advances the narrative and to lose all the nonessential material in between. Can you pare your

dialogue down to the critical middle—meaning the part that produces a change in the protagonist's situation?

CHAPTER 3: DIALOGUE TECHNIQUE

"So you're going to have to ask yourselves one simple question: Which one of us is speaking now?"

Jasper Fforde, *Lost in a Good Book*

In this chapter I will run through the basic dialogue techniques and procedures. I know many of these already may be familiar to you as a result of a lifetime of reading. But it's possible that, even though you've had your nose in a book constantly, you've never thought consciously about these dialogue details. And even if you have, a little review before the big test never hurt. Because nothing will make your manuscript appear more amateurish than the violation of one of these fundamentals.

Formatting Dialogue

Every time the speaker changes, start a new paragraph.

You've probably noticed that writers start a new graph every time the speaker changes. This allows the reader to understand that you've switched speakers, even before or without reading the attribution. Your goal is to minimize attributions to the maximum degree possible, and this is a tool that helps you do it. We don't need a constant repetition of "he said" and "she said" to tell us the speaker has changed. Formatting does it for you, at least some of the time.

There are rare occasions when writers will start a new paragraph while sticking with the same speaker, most commonly when a character is rattling on at length, lecturing some poor soul or soliloquizing. In this case, you omit the end quotation marks from the first paragraph but include the usual start quotation marks in the second paragraph. My advice is to keep this to a minimum. Long speeches will not accelerate the pace of your story. They tend to be boring. In the world of television, the rule of thumb is that no character can say more than two consecutive sentences before someone else speaks. That's because a back-and forth conversation is more engaging than a long sermon.

Another problem is that it's all too easy for readers to fail to notice the omission of the end quotation marks, so they incorrectly believe the speaker has changed. Once they get confused about who's speaking, they have to move backward and reread, trying to straighten it out in their minds. And you never want your readers to go backward. You want them to feel as if they are buoyed on a verbal tidal wave, moving forward at an exciting, breathless pace. So if you can avoid doing this (and you can), you should.

It has become trendy in some literary fiction, especially across the pond (or for Faulkner wannabes), to omit quotation marks, or even to omit indentation of paragraphs. Perhaps I'm just slow-witted, but I'm unable to see how this enhances anyone's reading experience. I've heard arguments that it makes the dialogue more immediate or more "real," but I frankly think that's a lot of nonsense. Quotation marks would've died out on their own if they impeded the reader's willing suspension of disbelief. Quotation marks exist because they perform a useful function—telling the reader when a character is speaking aloud. Eliminating that aid can only slow down the read. This pretentious device is a difference employed simply for the sake of being different. In other words, it's another one of those darlings that needs to be killed.

Punctuation goes inside the quotation marks.

Since we've decided to retain the quotation marks, let's also make it clear that your terminal punctuation, be it a period, question mark, exclamation point, or comma, goes inside the end quotation marks. This rule is universally observed (except on *Jeopardy!*, where the producers insist that putting punctuation inside the quote marks makes the clue confusing—but they try to avoid having the situation arise). This is easy to miss, especially when the end of the quote is the end of the sentence. But making this mistake will only make your manuscript seem amateurish and give the agent or editor reading it an easy excuse for moving on.

Don't confuse the end of the quote with the end of the sentence.

In many if not most cases, the quotation does not end the sentence. Often it is followed by the words "she said," or some variation thereof. In that instance, you put a comma at the end of the quote, followed by the end quotation marks, followed by "she said." This being the end of the sentence, the period goes after "she said," not at the end of the quotation. Please also note that in most word-processing fonts, opening quotation marks curve in a different direction than ending quotation marks. They are not interchangeable. Using the wrong marks will make your manuscript seem amateurish, and your word processing program may default to the wrong one in some circumstances, such as after a dash. If you upload an eBook formatted with this error, you will see a lot of carping on your Amazon page.

So a correctly written and punctuated sentence would read:

"What are you going to do now?" he asked.

But I would ditch the "he asked," because it's already obvious that this is a question and in context, the reader probably already knows who's asking it.

Dashes and Ellipses

First thing you need to get into your writer head is that both dashes and ellipses should be used sparingly, and you're hearing this from a guy who is currently in Dash and Ellipses Recovery. Yes, I have abused punctuation. I've binged on those dashes and ellipses. When people keep interrupting each other, it makes the dialogue move fast, and ellipses can reveal the emotion of the speaker without feeding it to the reader in adverbs. But like most useful writing tools, they can be overused. Limit yourself to maybe one per chapter. And make sure you use them correctly.

Dashes indicate an interruption. Ellipses indicate pauses, hesitation, or trailing off.

In real life, of course, people interrupt one another all the time, both purposefully and inadvertently. Copying this in fiction can show high emotion, anger, rudeness, arrogance, and can zip the pace along. But if you do it too much, it will start to be irritating. Don't make your readers long for a complete sentence.

A proper interruptive dash—as opposed to a hyphen—is usually created on most word processing programs by typing two hyphens together. You can set your preferences so the program automatically converts the two hyphens to a uniform line, the longer, unbroken em-dash.

Ellipses can also be skillfully used to indicate the dead air that helps work a joke or suggests a delayed reaction, a reticence, or contemplation. But if you do it too often, people will start skipping over it, which defeats the entire purpose.

The ellipsis is represented by three uninterrupted periods (...), but if it comes at the end of a sentence, you use four—three for the ellipsis and one to signify the end of the sentence.

Here's a demonstration of both tools being employed properly:

> "What do you have to say for yourself?" he asked.
> She thought for a moment. "I don't know. . . ."
> "Give me *something* to work with. Please."
> "If you would just give me a moment to think about it, I might say . . . I mean, if I were to be completely honest about it, I might—"
> "Great Caesar's Ghost! Just say it already."

Don't Play the Name Game

Here's an instance when what I'm recommending dovetails nicely with what happens in real-life—but not what I often see in the manuscripts of the pre-published. Normally, when you're having a conversation with people, you don't say their name over and over again. After all, you're right there looking at them. They know you're

23

talking to them. Why keep repeating their name? There's no good reason. And there's usually no good reason to do it in your fiction, either.

Avoid using character names in your dialogue—and attributions.

In most cases, before the dialogue begins, you've established who the players are. The reader knows who is talking to whom. So there's little reason to say their name repeatedly, either in the actual dialogue or in the attribution. Maybe you need to mention their name once in the narration to set the conversation up, and once again a page or two later to make sure no one gets confused. But you certainly don't have to do it every time they speak. Or even frequently. Readers like dialogue, and the fewer prose non-quote words that get in the way, the better.

How often do you need to remind the reader who's speaking to whom? That depends upon the book and the number of people in the conversation. If there are only two people talking to each other, you don't need to do it much at all. The indented paragraph tells the reader when you've switched from one speaker to the other, so the reader can follow the back and forth between them. If you have three or more speakers in the conversation, you may need to do it more frequently. But you still don't need to do it every time. Or anything close to every time.

Since people don't use names that often in real-life conversation, why do we see it so frequently in dialogue? David Morrell, my pal and a terrific writing teacher, thinks it's because writers copy television and movies. In those media, you will hear people frequently using the name of the party to whom they're speaking. ("What do you think we should do, Chet?") This is because visual media do not have a means of reminding viewers what the character names are—unless someone says it aloud. In a book, you can put the name in the description or the internal monologue or other non-dialogue parts of the story. If a reader forgets a character name, they can flip back a few pages and remind themselves. But you don't have that option at the Cineplex.

You don't need to do this—and you shouldn't. It will make your dialogue seem clunky and filled with repetitious and unnecessary information.

> "I don't believe a word you're saying, Morrie."
> "Well, Susan, I read it on the Internet, so it must be—"
> "Stop, Morrie. Just stop. Give it a rest."
> "As you wish, Susan."

Pretty bad, huh? Here's a passage I took from a manuscript, changing a few words around to protect the guilty:

> "Nora, I'm going for a smoke," Nick said.
> "Okay, Nick. But I wish you wouldn't," Nora whined.
> "You complain too much, Nora," Nick said.
> "It's just 'cause I love you, Nick," Nora replied.

Even if you took out all the attributions (and you could) this constant repetition of names would be boring and redundant. Try to eliminate them as much as possible.

One of the rare instances when I will have characters use the name of the person to whom they're speaking is when I have several characters in a conversation, I want to make clear who is about to speak, and I don't want to violate psychic viewpoint by using the viewpoint character's name. (If you don't know what I mean by psychic viewpoint, look at my book on Character.) So you don't want to use the character's name, but just saying "he" or "she" could lead to confusion because there are two or more characters of that gender. (In the third chapter of *Shine* I introduced eight characters, all female. Challenging? Don't get me started.) So I will have a character address a question or statement to the viewpoint character, using their name, so the reader knows the person named will reply without expressly being told. This is not ideal, but it's better than repetitious attributions or stage directions using the character's name, which will distance the reader from the viewpoint character. And I think it's somewhat justified, as you might well have to use someone's name in real life to make clear which member of a group you're addressing.

Highlights

1) Every time the speaker changes, start a new paragraph.

2) Punctuation goes inside the quotation marks.

3) Don't confuse the end of the quote with the end of the sentence.

4) Dashes indicate an interruption. Ellipses indicate pauses, hesitation, or trailing off.

5) Avoid using character names in your dialogue—and your attributions.

Red Sneaker Exercises

1) Scan the dialogue in your most recent writing project. Do you have character names in your dialogue? If so, can you eliminate some of them? Or all of them?

2) Practice using dashes and ellipses properly. Take the same dialogue passage and see how many times you can indicate interruption with dashes or indicate hesitation with ellipses. Does this quicken the pace? Now take out all the dashes and ellipses but one. Can you leave out some of the words you deleted to retain the snappy pace?

3) Find out how to use the Option or Preferences menu in your word processing program so that two consecutive hyphens will always be converted to em-

dashes. While you're there, you may discover other macros or shortcuts that will save time when you're writing fiction. Learn how to automatically indent new paragraphs without hitting the Tab key. Learn how to make the program automatically correct your most common typing errors.

CHAPTER 4: ATTRIBUTIONS

"Overuse [of attribution] at best is needless clutter; at worst, it creates the impression that the characters are overacting, emoting like silent film stars."

Howard Mittelmark

You may think I'm putting the cart before the horse when I discuss the attribution aspect of dialogue (the "he said" part) before I discuss the content of the dialogue. But I see pre-published writers making more fundamental errors in the attribution. Too often attributions are supplied too frequently, unnecessarily, or riddled with pointless stage directions and invasive adverbs. Attribution should be a simple matter, and in fact, usually works best when it's kept simple.

The simplest attribution is usually the best.

Dialogue Tags

More often than not, in fiction, the word that appears most frequently, after "a" and "the," is "said." This is good. This means there's lots of dialogue, and readers like dialogue. "Said" is a word with magical properties. Normally, I encourage writers to avoid word repetition. Not with "said." You can repeat "said" all you want and you will never stir my red pencil into action, because it's a word that doesn't much register with readers. You can use "said" all night long and readers rarely notice, because when their eyes scan the attribution, they focus on the name. When they read "Betty said," they realize that Betty is speaking. The quotation marks have already tipped them off that this is dialogue. So the word "said," though grammatically necessary, is essentially redundant.

And by the way, always use "Mary said" rather than "said Mary." To most readers, including me, "said Mary" seems awkward and non-idiomatic. In the English language, it always sounds more natural to put the noun before the verb.

Because readers don't register the word anyway, there is little reason to substitute "said" with synonyms or similar words. If it conveys useful information to the reader, fine. But if you're just doing it because you don't want to say "said" again—don't bother. And by all means, avoid the more exotic or esoteric substitutions. If your character is posing a question, I have no objection to using "asked" now and then. And if they're answering a question, I see nothing wrong with "replied"—occasionally. Don't overdo it.

Beyond that, the attributive words become more rarified, and thus, they should make fewer appearances in your book, if indeed they appear at all. After all, you're providing information the reader already has, and you don't want to throw in additional words that might slow the pace—the exact opposite of what dialogue is supposed to do. I can see an occasional reason for "demanded," "insisted," "shouted," and "screamed." Again, I emphasize *occasional*. All four stand out in a way that "said" never will, and all four come dangerously close to feeding the reader information they should be getting from the dialogue, not by having it force-fed to them in attributions. I could even see a rare use of "whispered" and "murmured." Maybe once a book.

DYNAMIC DIALOGUE

All too often in contemporary fiction, you'll read someone "hissing" dialogue.

"I'll hunt you down and terminate you!" she hissed.

And my response would be: How? You can't hiss a word, much less a sentence, unless it has a sibilant, that is, an "s" sound. And even when hissing is possible, it sounds rather melodramatic. Maybe okay for a Fu Manchu novel, but I wouldn't use it in one of mine.

I feel the same way about "growling":

"I'll hunt you down and terminate you!" she growled.

As David Morrell has pointed out, you can't growl a word, much less a sentence, unless it's in the lower register, that is, unless it moves down into your throat, like a guttural. This sentence actually goes up in pitch. Growling is not possible.

Similarly, humans don't bark (that's dogs) so let's eliminate "he barked," which is typically used as a substitute for "he yelled" by someone who has already used "yelled" and "shouted" and "screamed" too many times. Maybe you should just give your character a chill pill. Let's also ban "spitting" in attributions (and everywhere else). You can't spit words. Saliva, sure, words, no. So don't have your character "spit" their lines. Or rasp or rumble.

And by all means, eliminate the attributions that just suggest unintended jokes. Such as:

"Get away from that bomb!" he exploded.

Or worse:

"I love you!" he ejaculated.

Finally, please don't use tags that appear to be describing the way the dialogue is spoken, but actually provide information about the content.

"So I guess you've changed your mind," he chuckled.

Chuckling is something you do, not a way you speak. I don't know how you can chuckle words.

"Go away," he laughed.

Similarly, "laughed" is not a way of speaking dialogue, and it makes no sense with that line anyway, so this should be rewritten. Unless the incongruity is intentional. Here's one of my favorite lines from Raymond Chandler:

"Hello," she lied.

If you can eliminate these awkward crutches, your dialogue will seem more realistic and less over-the-top, not to mention easier to read, follow, and visualize. And you will be forced to improve the quality of your writing because you can't rely on these crutches.

You should especially avoid attributions if the information conveyed is already obvious (or should be).

"I'll track you down and murder you!" Nora screamed.

The dialogue itself suggests an agitated tone of voice, and if you missed that, the exclamation point tells you the same thing. "Screamed" is redundant and unwelcome.

Let's assume it isn't already obvious, but you do want the reader to understand that Nora is quite upset about this. A better, subtler approach might be to use a suggestive bit of description. So instead of:

"I've never heard anything so raunchy in my life," she said, embarrassed.

A better approach might be:

"I've never heard anything so raunchy in my life." Her cheeks were as crimson as her hair.

You see the difference? With the descriptive approach you create a visual image in the reader's mind. And you allow the reader to grasp your character's emotional state without having it fed to them. This is showing, not telling, which is always better. Readers are happier when they grasp the situation from the context.

Here are some more examples of bad attributions that provide information that should already be obvious:

"You'll never get away from me," her evil guardian sneered.

"No," he disagreed.

"Give it to me right now," she demanded.

Sometimes writers substitute bits of description for attribution. The idea is to provide the reader with information about who is saying what, but without the use of "said" or its brethren. This is why, in contemporary fiction, we see far too much of "Nancy smiled" or "Jack sighed" or "Karen grinned." Or blushed, inhaled, nodded, etc. Occasionally these non-attributive attributions may provide useful information. "He smiled" suggests happiness. "She nodded" indicates agreement. But too often writers use these indicators redundantly to tell the reader what they should have realized or what was already revealed in the dialogue.

"I agree. Totally," she affirmed, nodding her head.

See what I mean?

A little of this goes a long way and can end up being far more intrusive than "said." "Smiled," "nodded," "grinned" and a few others have become so overused as to be trite, so I now avoid them altogether. If your characters are engaged in a hardy, well-written convo, you don't need these attributions any more than you need traditional ones. Sometimes I think writers add them simply because they feel their characters have been talking too long, or there's been too much uninterrupted dialogue, so they need to break it up with a little non-dialogue. They are completely wrong. Please remember: readers love dialogue. Dialogue makes the story click along in an exciting, fast-paced manner. Can you have too much of such a good thing? Probably, but most writers will never come anywhere near that point.

This is equally true for more lengthy bits of stage direction (but note the discussion of "beats" in chapter 6).

Once upon a time, it seemed characters in novels were constantly smoking while talking. This meant writers could break up the dialogue with searching for a cig, searching for a match, fumbling with a lighter, drawing a deep drag, grinding it out in the ashtray, etc. Nowadays smoking is disfavored, so I read more protagonists walking to windows and staring out at the horizon, or pacing around desks, or fumbling with their cell phones. Either way, the point remains: these bits of aimless action are not necessary and do not enhance your dialogue. If there's no strong reason for your character to do something, don't have them do it.

Evil Thy Name is Adverb

In the nineteenth century and the early part of the twentieth, adverbs in dialogue attributions were common. They have now fallen out of favor and we are better for it. It's hard to pinpoint exactly when or why this happened, although many would give the credit to Hemingway. Papa became known for, among other things, expunging the adjectives and adverbs from his work and paring it down to the essential. In reality, if you read Hemingway closely, you'll find he did use some adjectives and occasionally even an adverb. But he didn't overdo it, and sometimes he disguised it by putting the adjectives someplace you wouldn't normally expect to find them, that is, not right in front of the noun they modify.

Whether you like Hemingway or you don't, his work has probably been more influential on subsequent writers than any other twentieth-century scribe. You can see his influence today, almost a hundred years later, and not only in literary fiction. Thrillermasters like Clive Cussler and his descendants still worship at the throne of Hemingway. And that means fewer modifiers, perhaps no adverbs at all. Especially in dialogue attributions.

Avoid adverbs in dialogue tags.

It's possible you might get away with one or two adverbs, but it's a slippery slope, and it doesn't take many to be too many, so I suggest training yourself not to use them at all. Once you've learned to live without them, perhaps you can allow yourself one or two, judiciously employed.

Here's a passage from a romance novel from a much earlier era.

> He said sulkily: "Oh, very well!" but, before suffering himself to be led away by Chris, took his leave of the Marquis, and said eagerly: "And you will take me to Soho, won't you, sir?"
>
> "If I don't, my secretary shall," replied Alverstoke haughtily.
>
> "Oh! Well - Well, thank you, sir! Only it would be better if you came with me yourself!" urged Felix insistently.
>
> "Better for whom?" demanded his lordship involuntarily.
>
> "Me," replied Felix, with the utmost candor.

Now you know how you *don't* want to write, yes? This excerpt is from *Frederica*, written by Georgette Heyer, who was also quite fond of tags like "asseverated" "interpolated" and yes, "ejaculated." She had many fans in her day, but that day is long past.

Too often, beginning writers will use adverbs to smuggle into their attributions information that should be in the dialogue. Or to put it another way, they're trying to compensate for the failings of their dialogue with adverbs, when of course what they should do is write more powerful dialogue.

"I'm afraid this isn't going so well," he said grimly.

You know what? If you rewrote that dialogue, it wouldn't be necessary to tell the reader it was said "grimly."

"We're finished. Doomed."

At this point, "grimly" would be redundant. We already got that.

"Keep working until you're done," he said harshly.

The problem is, the dialogue isn't harsh enough. Harsh it up, and then you don't need the adverb.

"You'll clean every tile till it shines like a diamond or I will have your head!"

See what I mean?

"I don't know what to do next," he said listlessly.

Don't tell, show. Make him sound listless.

"I just can't work up the energy to do anything any more."

Better. Write the dialogue correctly, and you don't need the adverb.

"I gave that creep the best days of my life," Nora said bitterly.

The adverb seems redundant because her bitterness seeps through every word of the dialogue. So I would cut it. But consider another possibility. What if you want to use the adverb to create an incongruity (like Chandler did), or to create surprise, or an unexpected twist?

"I gave that creep the best three days of his life," she said proudly.

Now you've used your adverbs to get your readers smiling. I might even permit a bit of stage direction, if it contributed something that couldn't be conveyed any other way.

"I gave that creep the best three days of my life." Nora squared her shoulders and straightened her back. "He wasn't worth it. He didn't deserve me."

Of course, the classic example of the transgressive use of dialogue-tag adverbs would be the Tom Swifties. These are named for the earliest incarnation of the Tom Swift "boys-adventure" books from the early part of the twentieth century, though to be fair, that was hardly the only place you could find excessive dialogue-tag adverbs. The freelance pseudonymous writers who churned out the Tom Swift books did tend to use adverbs to prop up limp dialogue. But it was others who came up with a way of using the adverbs to create a double meaning or a groan-inducing pun.

Here are a few of my favorites:

"I'll have a martini," said Tom, dryly.

"Who left the toilet seat down?" Tom asked peevishly.

"That's the last time I'll stick my arm in a lion's mouth," the lion-tamer said off-handedly.

"Can I go looking for the Grail again?" Tom requested.

"We just struck oil!" Tom gushed.

"They had to amputate both my ankles," said Tom defeatedly.

"We could have made a fortune canning pineapples," Tom groaned dolefully.

"I wish I drove a Scandinavian car," Tom sobbed. (It's a pun. Get it?)

"I stole the gold," Tom confessed giltily.

"3.14159265359...." Tom said endlessly.

Needless to say, I'm confident you can do better. Focus on the dialogue itself. Write great, vivid, purposeful dialogue that conveys both emotion and information in an economic but dramatic fashion. Let your characters talk about what matters to them in clever, absorbing ways that will capture your readers' imaginations. Then the attributions will take care of themselves, and probably will become largely unnecessary.

Highlights

1) The simplest attribution is usually the best.

2) Don't include an attribution unless it's necessary.

3) Use "said" substitutes sparingly.

4) Don't use the attribution to include information that should be obvious from the dialogue itself.

5) Don't break up the dialogue with pointless stage directions.

6) Don't have people speak in ways that words cannot be spoken.

7) Use adverbs in dialogue attributions sparingly, and only for a good reason.

8) Don't use Tom Swifties unless your goal is to make your reader laugh.

Red Sneaker Exercises

1) Try writing a scene between two characters without using any attributions. Invent a new situation (two people meeting for the first time in a singles bar works nicely) or rewrite a dialogue scene you've already got. See if you can write it without one speck of "he said" or other attributions, or stage directions, or adverbs. I bet you can. In fact, I bet it will be easier than you think.

2) Open one of your manuscripts and do a "Find" search for "-ly." Most of the words that come up will be adverbs. How many? Too many? Are some of them in dialogue attributions? Can you rewrite the dialogue so they become unnecessary?

CHAPTER 5: DIALOGUE TABOOS

"Of course I want to kill you," said Skulduggery. "I want to kill most people. But then where would I be? In a field of dead people with no one to talk to."

Derek Landy, *Kingdom of the Wicked*

When it comes to terminal punctuation, for dialogue or anything else, we writers have a paltry three choices: the period, the question mark, and the exclamation point. The quotation itself can end with a comma, if the attribution is yet to come. But that still leaves us with few options. So it's perhaps understandable that people might search for more. Or confuse or overuse the choices they have.

Ration Your Exclamations

Use exclamation points sparingly—if at all.
I don't know if you've ever known people who were constantly exclaiming, but I have, and I found them rather tiresome. Sort of like being chained to Robin Williams, 24/7. I generally prefer calmer souls. That goes for fictional characters, too. Don't let them exclaim all the time. It gets old. In comic books, at least once upon a time, sentences never ended with periods. In the hyperbolic world of four colors, sentences usually ended with exclamation points

(!!!), with the occasional question marks for questions or ellipses for calmer statements (…). (Which is a completely incorrect usage of the ellipsis, but never mind that). Evidently, in the superhero universe, life was always exciting. So there was never any need for calmer punctuation.

You may not be writing a comic book. So your characters probably don't need to be in a state of constant excitation. Too often, writers use exclamation points as a substitute for actually writing something exciting. If your situation and dialogue are exciting on their own, you don't need punctuation to get your reader's blood pumping. And if the dialogue isn't exciting, punctuation is not going to convince your reader that it is.

When I edit manuscripts in my small-group seminars, I cut exclamation points relentlessly. Rarely does one escape my red pen. And there is a reason for this. The first punctuation mark might have an impact on your reader, but if it keeps happening all the time, it will stop having any impact (much like the overuse of profanity, which is our next topic). You will not induce thrills with punctuation. But I constantly see people trying, in everything from thrillers, which are after all supposed to thrill, to children's books, which must be larger than life to capture a child's imagination.

If you want your dialogue to be exciting, write it that way. If you think your plot lacks thrills, start revising. But don't think for a minute that you can cure your manuscript's problems with exclamation points. I train people to write their entire novel without a single exclamation point. If they can discipline themselves in this way, forcing the excitement to come from the dialogue itself, then I figure they can probably allow one or two exclamation points to creep into the final draft. But no more. And if you've written the dialogue properly, you will understand that exclamation points are not only unnecessary, but may in fact detract.

"You slimy toad! I hate your stinking guts!" Nora exclaimed.

Overkill, huh? I think we already grasped that Nora was exclaiming. We didn't need two exclamation points, plus the word "exclaimed." (Note: "shouted" or "screamed' would've been little better.)

Now consider another approach.

"You slimy toad. I hate your guts." Her cold eyes never left his.

Wow. Now it's almost chilling, isn't it? Or at any rate, much improved. Here, instead of shouting at your reader, you're taking a more subtle approach. The result? Instead of sounding comic-booky, it induces goosebumps.

While we're talking about exclamation marks and dialogue, let me make three more points. No, you cannot have multiple exclamation points (!!!!!). The fact that someone might want to tells me that they've watered down the impact of exclamation points by overusing them.

Similarly, you cannot combine terminal punctuation marks, that is, end a sentence with both a question mark and an exclamation point.

"What do you think you're doing with that gun?!"

Sorry, no. I realize this sentence is capable of being considered both a question and an exclamation. Pick one punctuation mark or the other (probably the question mark). Trying to use both evidences insecurity, not to mention amateurism. Double terminal punctuation is not permitted by the style guides, and I don't think there are many publishing houses that would let you get away with it. Several decades ago, a well-known grammarian proposed the introduction of a new terminal punctuation mark: the interrobang. As you may have guessed, the interrobang was a hybrid with the head of a question mark and the base of an exclamation point, to be employed for those occasional sentences that were both.

Have you noticed that your keyboard does not have an interrobang? It could be inserted over the 6—who uses that carat anyway? But it isn't there because the interrobang never caught on, because we don't actually need it, and punctuation marks that serve no useful function do not survive long (so how long can it be before we expunge the semicolon?). Pick one or the other.

And finally, no you may not write your dialogue in all caps, or all bold, to indicate that your character is shouting, angry, or excited. Write your dialogue so the emotional state of your character is clear from the words. Choose your words carefully and correctly and you won't need cheesy keyboard special effects.

Let's take one sentence through all the possible permutations so you can see the difference for yourself.

"What am I going to do!" Nora shouted.

"What am I going to do?" Nora exclaimed.

"What am I going to do!!!!!"

"WHAT AM I GOING TO DO?"

"What am I going to do?" Nora's voice echoed through the room.

"What am I going to do?" Nora could barely get the words out.

"What am I going to do?" Red blotches marred her tear-stained face.

None of these is subtle, but I think they are definitely improved when they stop trying to use punctuation (or attributions) to create the excitement or tension that should stem from the dialogue.

Potty Mouths

Anyone writing dialogue set in the modern era will have to decide whether they will employ profanity, and if so, how much. Actually, this isn't even exclusive to those writing in the modern era. George R. R. Martin's Saga of Ice and Fire is replete with profanity, and very modern profanity at that, as are many future-day science-fiction novels.

This is a subject upon which reasonable minds can differ (like everything else in this book) so I will simply give you my opinion. When it comes to foul language, I think a little goes a long way. I can't say I've never used it—though I have in fact never used the words I find most foul and objectionable. When I do use profanity, I use it sparingly and to maximum effect. If someone is cursing all the time, it loses impact. But if a character swears once, in a field of otherwise unobjectionable language—readers take notice.

Use profanity sparingly and for maximum impact.

In *Capitol Conspiracy*, I had a character that was highly educated, intelligent, and well spoken. Most of the time, his dialogue read like what you would expect from the Harvard graduate he was. So you can imagine how it made readers' eyes widen when out of the blue, he turned to the Secret Service agent sitting beside him in Cadillac One and said, "Zimmer, how long have you been f***ing my wife?"

The language had even more sting because the character speaking was the President of the United States.

Now that to me was an instance of using profanity, once, to mean exactly what it means and to advance the story in a meaningful and dramatic way. To me, that works, and even if there is some reader out there who's offended, it's over quickly. Many times I've received mail complimenting me or thanking me for avoiding profanity. The truth is, I haven't avoided it altogether, but I've done it infrequently enough that it doesn't bother those with sensitive temperaments.

Contrast that with the approach you may have seen in other novels. How many times have you read dialogue like this?

> "If you don't bleeping get your bleep-bleeping hands off my bleep-bleeping wife this bleep-bleeping second, I'm going to grab you by the bleep-bleeping bleeps and nail them to the bleep-bleeping door."

Sadly—not an exaggeration. Where I see this most often is when relatively inexperienced writers portray lower-class or poorly educated characters (that they know nothing about), or sex workers, or sadly, police officers. The truth is, use of profanity has more to do with environment and education than it does social class, but even if the use of repeated profanity could be justified as "realistic," that does not mean you have to write that way. As I've said before, people don't turn to novels for realism. Indeed, part of the reason people turn to novels may well be the desire to escape this sort of repetitive boring language. I know that if I met someone who talked like that quotation, I'd run. So why would you think I'd want to read it?

Another reason I believe writers sometimes use excessive profanity is because they hear it in the movies. This is just as bad a reason to do it, because people read because they want something better than what they see on television or at the movies. People turn to books for a richer experience. So give it to them.

Another reason some writers use (or rationalize) profanity is that they think it will cause readers or critics to take their work more seriously. How sad is that? The truth is, critics often do make the grievous error of assuming that anything harsh, gritty, or negative, anything that shows people in their worst light, is somehow more realistic. This reflects a rather dim view of humanity, doesn't it? You might hear people arguing that cozy mysteries, like Agatha Christie's, are unrealistic, but hard-boiled mysteries, like Dashiell Hammett's, are more realistic. The truth is, neither has much to do with reality. Most reality is not nearly so interesting as a good book. But I absolutely reject this rather ugly notion that books portraying humanity at its worst—including the worst language—are more realistic.

Here's something that is reality: Readers expect writers to have a better command of the language than most of the regular Joes they bump into during the course of the average day. They turn to literature for sparkling dialogue and witty exchanges. They can get this bleep-bleeping language anywhere. I always told my children that resort to profanity is the sign of someone who has a poor vocabulary. Smart well-read kids ought to be able to come up with a better way to express themselves. I feel the same way about writers. Write something better.

By the way, if you're laboring under the misapprehension that the "f-word" is the worst or most offensive profanity you can put in a book, think again. In my experience, you will get far more angry mail if you use one of the many swear words or phrases that involve "using the Lord's name in vain." And the next-most likely to cause you problems are terms that are deeply insulting or offensive to women, such as the "b-word," followed by profanity laced with racism. I think a strong case can be made for avoiding all of these. There's almost always a better way to say it.

Some writers have found a middle ground by inventing their own profanity. This works particularly well for work set somewhere other than here and now. The excellent *Battlestar Galactica* reboot famously had its characters exclaiming "Frak!" The intended substitution was obvious, but this did solve the problem of getting expletives past censors and avoiding the alienation of any part of the audience.

In *Star Trek: The Next Generation*, Captain Jean-Luc Picard once exclaimed, "Merde." This never would've gotten past the censors, had he said it in English. Presumably the writers thought most viewers would not be able to translate. This show could get away with it because

Picard is from France (although apparently an odd region of France where everyone speaks with a British accent).

I have on occasion used profanity to make light of those who use profanity.

> Ben: I'm handling this case because I genuinely believe my client is innocent.
> DA: Bullshit.
> Ben: I think you rushed to judgment and didn't investigate thoroughly.
> DA: Bullshit.
> Ben: And I think your chief witness is hiding something.
> DA: Bullshit.
> Ben (jabbing him in the lapel): You need a thesaurus.

Slinging Slang

Slang is closely related to profanity. While readers may not be as immediately offended by slang, it offers the additional problems of dating a book and leaving some readers completely clueless about what your characters are saying.

Avoid slang terms that will date your book. Consider inventing your own slang if necessary or useful.

Elmore Leonard often invented slang for his crime-world characters. This solved two problems. First, it avoided language that some might find off-putting, and it also prevented the slang from making the book's characters seem passé. Nothing makes a book show its age more than characters spouting some long-dated patois, once hip, now comical. Slang changes with lightning speed. In the three decades I've been writing, I've seen many hip terms come and go.

In the early Ben Kincaid books, I tried to employ some then-contemporary slang for the two teenage girls living in Ben's boarding house. I soon learned better. In my more recent *Shine* series, I invented my own slang, for two specific reasons. First, the books are set about a decade in the future, so there's no reason to believe people would be using the same slang terms they do now. Indeed, perhaps because I was so immersed in this future world, when I tried it, most contemporary slang sounded quaintly archaic.

In *Shine*, a single act of time travel has effectively created an alternate timeline, a point of divergence between their world and ours. So I tried to come up with slang that would represent those changes and seem credible in that world. I later noticed many of the other authors writing in the *Shine* universe employed the same terms. In fact, some of them have told me the *Shine* slang crept into their real life. Text: "Oh my Gandhi. I just complained that this dull party was a total clownfest." They had instinctively adopted the *Shine* slang. Who knows, if that spreads, maybe someday this will be real slang.

In the science fiction series *Firefly*, the characters used a future-slang that was Asian-derived. This probably reflected how that world changed in the future, although if it was ever explained, I missed it. What this did most effectively was cause me to fail to understand a lot of the dialogue. I felt the series should come with a glossary. If your readers don't understand what your characters are saying, they will soon stop trying.

A Clockwork Orange did come with a glossary, but only in the American edition. Apparently the publisher thought

American readers needed that extra crutch. The author, Anthony Burgess, had two specific challenges. He had to bring a future society to life, and he had to do it primarily with young rebellious characters—in other words, those most likely to use trendy slang. So Burgess invented his own and it works wonderfully well. There may be brief moments when the reader doesn't immediately know what the characters are saying, but it can usually be deduced from the context, and the fact that the characters speak in this undeniably different manner makes the book all the more compelling. (*Clockwork Orange* was a major influence for *Shine*.)

I don't think it's the end of the world if you drop a bit of slang into your manuscript, but as with the profanity, don't overdo it. If your character is a Valley Girl, you can drop a "like" or "you know what I'm saying" into the conversation every now and again just to remind the reader who this person is. But keep it to a minimum. Even though in reality that character might say it all the time, in fiction, it will become annoying quickly. And even if your character might be rather annoying in reality, that's unacceptable in fiction. Annoying characters tempt the reader to read something else.

Phonetics

One of the most difficult situations for a writer is dealing with the dialogue of a character that speaks in a foreign language, or with a foreign accent, or an American accent or dialect other than standard Midwestern, nighttime-news English. You want to suggest the difference in pronunciation without doing anything that slows down or irritates the reader. What's the solution?

The answer will vary from book to book. Some books, and some readers, may be more tolerant of dialogue that requires a little extra effort. But there are limits, even in the most rarified or intellectual fiction.

First of all, if you can avoid this problem altogether, do. Avoidance may not seem like much of a solution, but sometimes retreat is the better part of valor. I particularly would suggest that if you are a new and relatively inexperienced writer, this is a challenge you can save for later in your career, when you have a few million more words under your belt. There is no book that suffered because all its characters spoke with readily comprehensible American speech patterns.

If you're determined to incorporate a foreign language into your dialogue, do it sparingly. Books do not have subtitles. I suppose you could put English translations into the footnotes, but who would want to read a book where the text has incomprehensible gibberish and you have to go to the footnotes to find out what's being said? Sadly, sometimes writers use those online translators that invite you to type in your English language sentence to receive a foreign language translation. Most simply implement a word-for-word substitution process that may result in a sentence that is far from accurate.

A better approach would be to simply *suggest* the foreign language every now and again. You've probably read books where the Russian character occasionally says "Nyet!" or the bayou character says "ain't," just to remind the reader who they are. This may be less than realistic, but it serves a purpose, and it doesn't slow down the reader. Always remember—dialogue should be the easiest part of the book to read. Realistic or not, this is a better approach than requiring the reader to translate dialogue. And it is certainly an improvement over all those PBS programs where foreign nationals still speak English, but with an accent. Or *Doctor Who*, where every alien in the universe speaks with a tony British accent.

Dialect presents a special problem, because writers are so often tempted to write it phonetically. Could anything be more tiresome to read? I have heard readers state flat-out that they will not read a book in which dialogue is written phonetically. I'm sympathetic. In those books, the part of the novel that should be the easiest to read becomes the most difficult.

Yes, I know Mark Twain did it (brilliantly) in *The Adventures of Huckleberry Finn*, but that was a different era and a completely different situation. At that time, most books were not written in the language of the people, but rather in the language of the university. Reread Melville and Emerson and see if I'm not right. In *Huck Finn*, Twain had his Hannibal, MO characters speak the way he remembered people there actually speaking—and it was revolutionary. People were willing to translate the dialogue because this was a new and exciting idea. It didn't hurt that Twain was already immensely popular or that the book was so good, so relevant, striking right to the heart of the American identity. And remember—Huck apologizes for his poor language at the start of the story.

A better approach is to use phonetics sparingly, just as you did with profanity and slang, to suggest a way of speaking rather than to precisely reproduce it. So instead of letting a character rattle on and on with stuff like:

"Dinja know he wuz gunna getcha?"

restrict yourself to:

55

"Didn't you know he was gonna get you?"

If the reader already understands who this character is, they may not need constant reminders. And if they need it at all, it will be when the character is introduced, not throughout the entire book. A simple suggestion is sufficient to remind your reader of the character's illiteracy or stupidity or dialect or whatever it is you're trying to convey. If you read an author who is ferociously good at this, like James M. Cain, you'll see that choosing the right word and syntax is more important than exact phonetic duplication.

One word can go a long way—without sucking all the fun out of the dialogue. In the Ben Kincaid novels, I occasionally had the street-smart but not formally educated investigator, Loving, drop his "g"s at the end of "-ing" words. Or say "gonna." Or "kinda." But I drew the line there. If you write the dialogue properly, the reader should grasp who the character is without requiring a phonetic crutch.

Talking to Yourself

Sometimes people ask whether I think reading work aloud while revising is a good idea. My answer is: It depends upon why you're doing it. If you're doing it to "sound-check" whether the dialogue sounds right or sounds realistic, then my answer is a decided no.

Here's the problem: When you read your own work, you will use inflection and tone and pacing to make the dialogue sound exactly how you want it. But those tools aren't on the printed page. When your readers read your book, they will not have the benefit of your voice to suggest inflection, pace, where the emphases should go, where to speed up and where to slow down. Your novel will not be printed with margin notes for subvocalizing readers. So the test isn't whether you can make it sound good. The test is whether it reads right. And the only way you can determine that is by reading it the same way your reader will—with a blank-slate brain, silently.

Reading your dialogue aloud is not the best way to determine whether it works. Better to read it slowly and silently, trying to reproduce the experience of the reader.

I have occasionally heard people say that reading dialogue aloud helps them root out dialogue that sounds phony or artificial. I'm dubious about this, but if it works for you, fine. But make sure you're not simply indulging yourself, reveling in the loveliness of your own pretty words, or subconsciously preparing for your future book reading at Barnes & Noble.

Some experienced writers have told me that reading aloud helps them during the editing process. I will discuss this more in the book on Editing, but generally speaking, anything that gets you away from the electronic screen and causes you to read more carefully, focusing on each and every word, is probably a good practice. After having over twenty audiobooks recorded from my work, I finally had the opportunity to sit in the studio during the recording of *Shine*. This was both an enjoyable and enlightening experience (especially since the voice artist was ferociously inventive and talented). More than once during the recording, I heard a line that didn't sound right to me. Fortunately, since the book hadn't been published yet, I could fix it. So I can grudgingly see the value of hearing your work read aloud, but don't let that be the primary means of checking your dialogue. Make sure it works for readers who won't hear you or anyone else read it aloud.

Highlights

1) Use exclamation points sparingly—if at all.

2) Use profanity sparingly—if at all.

3) Use slang sparingly—if at all.

4) Use phonetic spellings sparingly—if at all. (Are you detecting a pattern?)

5) Reading your dialogue aloud is not the best way to determine whether it works. Read it slowly and silently, trying to reproduce the experience of the reader.

Red Sneaker Exercises

1) Take an exciting action-packed chapter from your work-in-progress and see if you can rewrite it using no exclamation points. After you've accomplished that, pick one place where you might judiciously choose to insert an exclamation point. Do you find that it does its job even more so because exclamation points aren't littered all around the chapter? Now try the same experiment with profanity.

2) Is your book riddled with slang terms that are likely to pass out of fashion? (Even writers like Shakespeare and Dickens did). If so, can you eliminate or replace them? Do you have a coterie of characters who might employ their own slang or group patois?

59

3) If you have characters employing phonetically spelled dialogue to suggest dialect or foreign language, consider eliminating them. If you can't do that, consider ways of making the dialogue tolerable by suggesting the differences without hammering the reader over the head with them.

CHAPTER 6: DIALOGUE CHOREOGRAPHY

It is such a complex matter we live within, it is impossible to track logic and decision-making really, so therefore each choice can actually only be seen as coincidence.

Alva Noto

One of the hardest aspects of writing dialogue is balancing the talking part with the action part. Although writers sometimes underestimate how long a book can proceed with pure dialogue, it's undeniable that at some point you should intersperse some non-dialogue narrative to give the reader a break, to interrupt long speeches, or simply for the sake of variety. Finding the proper balance between dialogue and narration can be one of the most challenging parts of writing fiction.

The Beat Goes On

Beats are bits of action interspersed throughout a dialogue passage.

Many times you've read dialogue interrupted when the character walks to the window, or lights a cigarette, or removes his glasses and rubs his eyes. Earlier I called this "stage direction," but the technical term is "beats." (Note:

If you read the book on Structure, you found the term "beat" employed in an entirely different manner. Sorry. That "beat" comes from Hollywood, where they are not always renowned for innovation.) Usually, these beats involve physical gestures or motions, but brief spurts of interior monologue can also be used in much the same manner.

Here's an example of action beats at work:

Kadey woke, rolled over to the other side of the immense bed, and whispered into Madeline's ear. "I'm awake."

"Me too." Madeline pulled the covers closely around her body. "Are you cold? I'm cold."

"I had the most bizarre dream." She closed her eyes. "It was so spooky."

"Tell me about it."

She rolled over. "I don't know if I should."

Madeline picked up the pillow and whacked her sister in the face. "You tease. You can't say you had a weird dream and then not tell me anything about it. Spill already. I want to hear every single detail."

First of all, you probably noticed that there's not a single "she said" in the entire passage. It isn't necessary. The beats, combined with the fact that the conversation is an obvious back-and-forth between two characters, make it easy to follow who's speaking without obvious dialogue tags. The beats also provide information about the two girls, their relationship, and their emotional states. Best of all, despite the beats (probably more than necessary), this still feels like a dialogue passage and retains the rapid pace of a dialogue passage.

Here's an example of not only action beats but also internal monologue:

Alan stood behind the cash register. "May I take your order?"

The beautiful brunette barely noticed him. "I want some food."

No joke. *Thank you for that fascinating fact. I thought you came to the restaurant for spare tires.* "What would you like?"

"I don't know what I'm in the mood for."

And you're expecting me to tell you? "Hamburgers are on sale today."

"Eew. Meat is gross. I'm a vegetarian."

He tried to control his facial expression. He knew when he was irritated he had a tendency to let it show. Although in this case, his eyes could probably pop out of his head and this chick wouldn't notice. "There's no meat in French fries."

"They're fattening."

"Everything is."

Here we have some traditional action beats—i.e., positioning poor Alan behind the cash register—but most of the beats take the form of Alan's internal thoughts or monologue. These beats serve two purposes. First, they provide information about Alan's character and his emotional state. They also keep the reader squarely posited in Alan's viewpoint. In a rapid-paced dialogue exchange, it's possible for a reader to get lost. Internal thoughts do not need to appear before every line of dialogue, but it does keep the reader oriented properly. And this is fun for the reader, because they get to hear something the difficult woman at the counter does not. This leaves readers feeling as if they're on the inside track.

Please also note that internal thoughts come in two flavors—dialogue-like passages written as if the character is speaking aloud (*Thank you for that fascinating fact*), and narrative passages that tell us what the character is thinking (He tried to control his facial expression.). The former do not have to be put in italics. You can, if you like, but the reader should be able to tell that it's internal monologue without this indicator. To me, the excessive use of italics is just as tiresome as the excessive use of anything else.

Since you've heard me say at length that readers love dialogue and don't mind long passages of dialogue, you may be wondering why you would want to introduce beats at all. I advise writers not to write a descriptive passage without a valid purpose. Much the same here. Don't do the beat unless it serves a constructive purpose other than quelling your insecure fear that the dialogue has gone on too long.

Here's my list of good and valid reasons for introducing beats:

1) As a substitute for monotonous or intrusive dialogue tags;

2) To lend variety to the pacing of the dialogue passage;

3) To subtly provide the reader with information about a character's emotional state;

4) To reinforce or tie the dialogue to the character or the setting; and

5) To suggest a change in a character's thinking or emotional direction.

DYNAMIC DIALOGUE

In the two examples provided above you can see how beats vary the pace of the dialogue (perhaps more than is necessary) and as a substitute for "he said" and "she said." You can also see beats quietly nudge the reader into remembering where this scene is located. In visual media such as television, this is not necessary, because the viewer can see perfectly well where the characters are. Readers may need occasional reminders, especially for longer scenes. In the second example, I presume an earlier sentence introduced the fact that Alan is working in a fast-food restaurant. Mentioning that he's standing behind the cash register is just a way of reminding the reader.

Emotional Status Report

In the world of screenplays, writers often label dialogue as "on-the-nose" or "off-the-nose." And contrary to what might be your first guess, off-the-nose is usually better. With on-the-nose dialogue, the character says exactly what they're thinking or feeling. With off-the-nose dialogue, they say something more indirect or seemingly off-topic, but which nonetheless gives the reader an indication of what the character is thinking or feeling.

The preference for off-the-nose dialogue is much like my preference for showing rather than telling. This is true not only in novels but in screenplays. When an actor's line is "I'm sad," it seems obvious and, frankly, boring. From the standpoint of the actor playing the part, it's less challenging than an off-the-nose comment which, coupled with fine acting, suggests the true emotional state. (Only major hambones want more dialogue. First-rate actors want less to say and more to do.) Similarly, dialogue can be used to subtly give an indication of someone's emotional condition without stating it so overtly and obviously that it makes little impact on the reader.

Here's an example:

> Beth peered over the rim of her coffee cup. "I think maybe this year we shouldn't put up a Christmas tree."
>
> Her husband did not look up from his newspaper. "I thought you loved putting up the tree. You always make such a big deal about it."
>
> "And I don't think anyone cares but me." She took a long drag from her mug. "Especially now that the kids are gone."
>
> "What about the stockings? The Christmas lights."
>
> "I can do without them, too."
>
> "The wreaths? The crèche?"
>
> "Why bother? Better to start fresh."
>
> He laid down his paper. "And me?"
>
> She held the mug in both hands, treasuring the warmth.

Okay, so subtle really isn't my best thing. But this is an example of getting character information across without overtly saying it. Exactly how much subtlety you can get away with depends upon your estimation of your audience, but generally speaking, I think readers are smarter than writers realize. Why else would they still be reading books, when there are so many easier ways of absorbing stories? Let the reader have the pleasure of feeling smart, feeling that they're savvy enough to read between the lines. That comes from writing off-the-nose dialogue that suggests without telling.

Shifting Directions

Beats can be a fabulous tool for cluing the reader into a shift in the character's intellectual or emotional state, perhaps an important step forward in the character arc. Remember, readers will enjoy it more and remember it longer when they feel they got it on their own. What they intuit gives them a warm feeling of satisfaction. What they are told makes little impact.

Here's an example:

"Don't even bother trying to change my mind," David said. "It isn't possible."

Sadie's eyes burned into his soul. "You said you'd do anything for me."

"That was a long time ago."

"You said every day with me was like an eternity in paradise."

"I was drunk with love."

"You said your entire universe revolved around my face."

Would this woman never quit? She was the one who ended it. Why should he be made to feel guilty? "This is really quite futile. So if you'll excuse me—"

"I'm going to have a baby."

His hand flew to his face and the air conditioner suddenly seemed incredibly loud.

This is neither deathless prose nor particularly subtle, but I hope you can see what I'm describing. The narrative needs to suggest how the news has registered with David, and how his attitude is about to shift. But we can imagine that without having it shoved down our throats. The suggestion made with the beats—transitioning from his arrogant internal monologue to his hand covering his face—is sufficient. In fact, the scene is stronger because we are shown the change rather than told it.

Highlights

1) Beats are the bits of actions interspersed through a scene.

2) Beats typically involve physical action or gestures, but they can also involve a character's internal thoughts.

3) Beats should do one of the following (and if they don't, take them out):

a)   Replace monotonous or intrusive dialogue tags;
b)   Lend variety to the pacing of the dialogue;
c)   Subtly provide the reader with information about a character's emotional state;
d)   Reinforce or tie the dialogue to the character or the setting; and
e)   Suggest a change in a character's thinking or emotional direction.

Red Sneaker Exercises

1) Work through the five purposes for beats and see if you can accomplish all of them, basing your examples on a passage from your work-in-progress. Can you get the emotional point of the scene across without stating it overtly?

2) See if you can write an entire stretch of dialogue without attributions. Instead, use beats. And don't use beats any more than necessary. Are you able to make it clear

who's speaking? Are you able to bring the scene fully to life?

3) See if you can write an entire scene using beats you've never used before. Better yet, see if you can write a scene using beats no one has used before. Come up with your own. Too many writers overuse trite indicator-beats. Can you come up with a better beat?

CHAPTER 7: CHARACTER CHARISMA

"You can't handle the truth!"

A Few Good Men

Dialogue can provide information to your reader in a manner that is less likely to slow down the story. But don't limit yourself to that, or overdo it. Dialogue is your chance to let your characters speak with their own voice, to bring the story to life with emotion and immediacy. So don't let it be a dumping ground for stuff you can't fit in anywhere else. Let your dialogue sparkle and shine.

Exposition is for Losers

I still remember the gasping I heard the first time I stood before a crowd and said these fateful words: Exposition is for losers. (If you're curious, this talk is recorded on the *Fundamentals of Fiction* DVD.) Gasping, frowning, rumbling, followed by confusion. If that's true, the crowd wondered, how do we reveal our characters' backstories, which we have worked in detail like you told us to, mister, in your lecture on Character?

And the answer is: Maybe never. The point of understanding your characters' backstory is so you can write the characters better, not so you can do some gigantic infodump and unload it on the reader. And yes, as I explained, putting some of that info in a dialogue passage might be better than endless narrative exposition. But it's not the highest and best use of dialogue.

Before I embarked on the first Ben Kincaid book, I worked out Ben's background in detail (and no, it isn't all autobiographical). This turned out to be a wise investment, since I'm still writing that character periodically many years later. But I didn't dump everything I knew in *Primary Justice*, the first book in the series. You got what you needed to know about Ben's relationship with his father, because that played a significant role in Ben's character arc in that book. Even then, many of the salient details of that destructive relationship were not revealed until the sixth book, *Naked Justice*. There are also references in *Primary Justice* to Ben's previous romantic relationship, the one that did him so much damage, involving a woman named Annie. And although a few clues were dropped along the way, my readers didn't get the full story on that one—even though I knew it all along—until the fourteenth book, *Hate Crime*.

This is not all a function of me being cagy with my readers, or building mystery through unanswered character questions. I revealed information that related to that particular book and held back information that did not. I told Annie's story when it mattered. Until then, it would've simply been extraneous infodump—even if I put it in dialogue.

Backstory and exposition may be more tolerable in dialogue—but don't overdo it.

You may have read books that had passages more or less like this:

"Hey, George, remember that time we stole the eagle from the engineering building and Old Man Perkins ended up giving us detention and that's how we became friends?"

"Oh yeah. And now here we are working together and we have to figure out a way to steal the top-secret report from the CDC safe or your completely innocent patient is going to jail. I don't know how we're going to get that thing in time."

He snapped his fingers. "Maybe we'll do it the same way we stole that eagle, all those years ago!"

Okay, maybe you've never read a passage quite that bad. But you know what I'm talking about. In this passage, we have a lot of recap and revelation smuggled into dialogue. We have both backstory—filling the reader in on stuff that happened before the narrative began—and exposition—providing the reader with background information so they can understand what's going to happen next. It's clumsy and awkward and, frankly, bad writing. One sentence might've been acceptable. But this is way too much, too fast.

In your typical television drama, you can see the relationship between exposition and action worked out with formulaic regularity. Right after the commercial break, the characters, be they cops or CSIs or PIs or what have you, get together for a fast-talking confab about what they've learned, usually through amazingly effective off-screen research (off-screen presumably because watching people research and do actual detective work would be so boring. The great exception was *Buffy the Vampire Slayer*, where the central meeting place was the library and almost every episode saw the Scoobies poring through old books. No wonder I loved that show.) And then, once the new information has been announced, the characters go into action, because today most hour-dramas are more about action than clever dialogue. At the end of the action sequence they encounter some game-changing surprise— gasp!—so you won't change the channel during the commercial. After the commercial, there's another brief regroup while they reveal what they've learned this time...and so on.

You don't want to imitate television. You have tools the teleplay scenarist does not, such as narrative prose and internal monologue. You can reveal information in more interesting ways than having people announce it. You can show the deliberative process.

Every crime story will have a scene in which the lead character interviews one suspect or another seeking information. This is going to be a dialogue scene. Information will be revealed. Some of it may be red herrings, but it is still information and it moves the story forward, even if the information turns out to be misdirection (as in virtually every conversation for the first four-fifths of the mystery). This is exposition through dialogue.

The same is true for courtroom scenes. The lawyers give speeches to the jury. The jury talks back during *voir dire*. The lawyer quizzes the witnesses. The other lawyer objects, which means they all get to argue, until the judge resolves the conflict. You can have accusations, surprise revelations, horrifying forensic reports, tattletales, quislings, and the tragically faithful. And since lawyers tend to be well spoken and reasonably intelligent, it's usually pretty good arguing. Which culminates in more speechifying from the lawyers— until at last, the jury...speaks.

The point is, it's all dialogue. Wall-to-wall dialogue. Sure, you can introduce the beats and perhaps the occasional revelatory piece of evidence. But it's still all dialogue. And readers love it.

Not every scene takes place in a courtroom. What seems natural in court would seem forced and unnatural somewhere else. In most cases, you want more variety. Some information can be provided in dialogue, but some should also come from action scenes, from interior monologue (particularly good for hinting at character backstory), and from character contemplation.

Try to use the techniques discussed in the next chapter—characters working on separate agendas, characters clearly withholding information, sarcasm, mistrust, personal history, and others to make it more interesting than the rapid-fire infodumps you see on television.

One more note: Dialogue can be a great tool for revealing information without letting your reader understand its significance, because you, the infinitely clever writer, have disguised it as something other than what it is. Misdirection is the great art of the mystery writer, but every good story should have some mysteries buried within. Searching for the unknown is what inspires readers to keep turning pages.

In my book *Naked Justice*, the sister of the murder victim, on the witness stand, mentions in passing that her sis was reading Medea at the time of her death. She was trying to demonstrate how much smarter her sister was, and most readers never take it to be anything more than that. But in fact, I planted a major clue to the solution of the case (which I am not going to explain in any greater detail, because, hey, you might want to read this book someday).

So the reader isn't tipped off, but when the time comes to explain all, readers remember the clue they didn't pick up on. Readers slap their foreheads with a feeling of surprise and pleasure because the clues were provided fairly but you nonetheless managed to surprise them.

Finding the Right Voice

It's axiomatic in the world of writing that every character should have his or her own voice, which means one character should sound different from another. Dialogue should not be interchangeable. If you reversed the order of a conversation and switched the attributions, it wouldn't sound right. It would sound as if one character were speaking another's words.

Every character should have a distinctive voice.

This is something that's easy to say and oh so hard to bring off. This requires you to know your character inside out, including, obviously, how they talk. People with different backgrounds will speak differently. Even people with similar backgrounds may speak differently. Do you speak just like your sister? Or your mother? Probably not. There may be some similarities, but there will be even greater differences. You must be sensitive to these differences and learn to develop your ear for the way people talk.

How do you develop this inner ear?

You learn to listen. This is a trait of all great writers, especially when it comes to dialogue. Writers are people who listen far more than they talk. Writers are people who pay close attention to what people do and how they do it, storing away details for when they need them. Writers are the ones who sit in restaurants eavesdropping on the conversation at the table behind them because it's more interesting and might be just the thing for some character you write somewhere down the line. Spend time listening to people, not only to what they say, but to how they say it. And what they don't say.

When you write your dialogue, especially when you're revising, don't focus only on what information your character must convey. Think about how they should say it. The conversational style should match their personality. The vocabulary should match their education and experience.

This may not be possible for every character in your book. You may avoid detailed characterizations for minor characters because they're minor and you don't want to mislead the reader into thinking otherwise. A spear-carrier who is only going to make a brief appearance probably does not need a dramatically different way of speaking.

This is just a rule of thumb, but your average novel has five or six major characters and dozens of minor ones. Those five or six major characters should each have a distinctive manner of speech, so much so that if you took their dialogue out of context and put it on a page by itself, a reader should still be able to identify which character said that. This is not as difficult as I'm making it sound. But it does require you to understand who your characters are.

Let me give you an example. Ben Kincaid and his legal assistant/law partner Christina McCall have been the two lead characters throughout the series. But they are not the same person. Indeed, following the time-honored principle that contradictions are more interesting than correspondences, Ben and Christina are very different. Both are smart, true, but Ben is more intellectual and book-smart, while Christina is more common sense and street-smart. Ben is reserved and awkward around others. Christina is socially outgoing and more comfortable in public. Christina is more naturally aggressive, but Ben is perhaps more tenacious. And Ben always tries to do what he perceives as the ethically correct thing to do, while Christina has a more pragmatic approach.

Are these differences reflected in the way they talk? Of course they are.

With Ben, you're more likely to get long words, legal terminology, euphemisms, sly wit, musical quotations (he was a music major, after all), and the occasional conversational stutter reflecting his natural reticence. With Christina, you're more likely to get shorter words, simpler but more direct expressions, straight talk, in-your-face sarcasm and, especially in the early books, faux-French phrases, an obvious over-compensation for her relative lack of education. (She went back to school about halfway through the series). All these factors must be reflected in the characters' dialogue, not just occasionally, but every time they speak.

I recommend writers dedicate an entire draft to polishing dialogue, and a big part of that polish should be making the dialogue *sound* right. There are obvious overt short cuts to making characters sound different, such as having a character repeatedly drop French phrases, or repeatedly tell lawyer jokes, or repeatedly employ Native American terminology (all rookie approaches to dialogue distinction I employed in my first book, when I didn't know any better). But better and subtler distinctions will arise from paying close attention to matters of vocabulary and grammar and syntax, listening to the natural rhythms of conversation, and understanding the way people talk.

DYNAMIC DIALOGUE

What's the Key to Writing Interesting Dialogue?

This is another occasion when the answer to the question seems so simple you may start to wonder why you're reading this book (but of course, simple is not the same as obvious). There are many different approaches and techniques discussed in this book, and I hope you will try all of them and see if they work for you. See if they make your book better than it was before. But at the end of the day, there's only one sure way to make your characters' dialogue interesting.

Give your characters something interesting to say.

Simple, right? And yet oh so often forgotten by people writing books, sometimes even people with lots of experience who should know better. You can inject all the style and wit and exclamation points you want into your dialogue. It will still fail if you haven't given your characters anything noteworthy to say. Grab the reader's attention. Even the dullest but necessary infodumps can be enlivened if they are written well. Look for clever and unexpected ways to reveal information. Inject your conversations with tension and subtext (discussed in the next chapter). What's going on in this conversation? What are the characters really thinking? What conflicts lie just below the surface, perhaps hinted at in the conversation but never fully revealed or explained? Adding additional layers to the conversation is the best way to make it riveting.

Some distinctions are better than others. In the world of *Star Trek* (I'm contractually obligated to mention *Star Trek* at least twice each book), both Spock and Data failed to use contractions. Spock is not speaking his first language (he's from the planet Vulcan), and Data's positronic brain has a programming flaw that prevents him from understanding contractions. Does this make sense? He can juggle google-size numbers in his head and theorize about quantum mechanics without trying hard, but contractions baffle him. Sure.

There's a reason why the writers wrote dialogue for these characters without contractions. They wanted to remind you that these characters are not human. The special effects budget didn't permit anything other than human actors with a bit of makeup, so the writers made their dialogue sound slightly stilted and formal to remind you that they aren't human beings. A simple fix, and one that never became obtrusive.

Compare their dialogue with that of Yoda, in the *Star Wars* films. His dialogue is also written in a somewhat unnatural way to remind you that he's not human. He may look like a Muppet and sound like Miss Piggy, but he's actually an alien creature from Dagobah. And as such, you'd think he might speak another language, but no, he speaks English. Just weirdly. The weirdness of Yoda's dialogue comes from inverting the natural subject-verb-object word order of English language sentences. For Yoda, the object or verb is flipped before the subject. "Powerful you have become." And so forth.

Unfortunately, Yoda's dialogue sounds so odd that, for me anyway, it usually required some mental translation that caused me to miss some of it, at least the first time I saw the film. Whenever Yoda has something really important to say, however, something George Lucas wants to make sure you get, Yoda goes back to normal subject-verb-object order. "The fear of loss is a path to the Dark Side." Or "A Jedi uses the Force for knowledge and defense, never for attack." Screen *The Empire Strikes Back* tonight and see if I'm not right.

DYNAMIC DIALOGUE

Surprises are good for making dialogue interesting, too. Unexpected developments. Unexpected reactions to unexpected developments. Something different. Something your readers haven't seen before. Grab your reader's attention. And never let it go.

Highlights

1) Backstory and exposition may be more tolerable in dialogue—but don't overdo it.

2) Every character should have a distinctive voice.

3) The best way to make your characters interesting is to give them something interesting to say.

Red Sneaker Exercises

1) Identify the biggest backstory issue in your book. What crucial bit of information does the reader need to know that occurred prior to the first page of the book? Make sure that doesn't get revealed too early. Make sure there are no flashbacks in the first half of the book. Then see if you can write a little dialogue—a *little* dialogue—that makes expository narration or flashback unnecessary.

2) Pull a page from your manuscript at random and read the first snatch of dialogue you encounter. Would you be able to tell who was speaking even if you didn't already know, based upon your understanding of the characters? If not, what tags or jargon or vocabulary could you add to make that dialogue more distinctive? Now spot-check the dialogue of the other major characters. How can you make it unique, or more emblematic of the character delivering the line?

3) Can you make your dialogue more interesting, sparkling, inventive, or witty? Is one of your characters a smart aleck?

4) What do you think is most distinctive about the way you talk? Can you inject that element into one of the characters

CHAPTER 8: TEXTURED DIALOGUE

Good dialogue illuminates what people are not saying.

Robert Towne

Every book needs tension. Every scene needs tension. So as you might guess, every dialogue exchange also needs tension. Tension is the lurking sense that something is not right with the world, that things are not as they should be. The reader knows a character is experiencing tension when their emotions are in conflict with one another.

When the path is clear, there's no tension, even if the character has not accomplished all they would like. Tension is best when the character thinks, "I don't want to do this—but I must," or perhaps, "I'm going to do this, but I know there will be disastrous consequences." When the reader feels that dichotomy lurking beneath the surface, tugging a character in opposing directions, it results in a textured multi-level reading experience, or to put it more simply, a gripping read.

In his famous Nobel Prize-acceptance speech, William Faulkner said the best drama is about "…the human heart in conflict with itself." And one of the best ways to bring that conflict to life, to inform the reader about those emotional struggles, is through skillfully written dialogue.

Dialogue with Punch

The best dialogue has emotional impact.

When you write your dialogue, you should try to move your story forward, first and foremost. But the best dialogue will do much more. Dialogue that does nothing but provide information and fulfill its plot function will likely seem flat, wooden, and unmemorable. When you write dialogue with real emotional impact, you'll make your reader laugh or cry, feel their heart beat faster, and vicariously experience adventure, romance, or resolution.

Here are some strategies for adding texture to enrich your dialogue.

The Soul of Wit

Earlier in this book I discussed the value of injecting humor into your dialogue. But there are many ways to accomplish this, from elaborate parodies to zippy one-liners.

Humorous dialogue enlivens almost any scene.

The Zinger. Who doesn't enjoy a snappy comeback? *Mad Magazine* used to devote entire books to them (*Snappy Comebacks to Stupid Questions*). Even if you think your book is too serious or literary for overt humor, or you think the situation is too dire for the characters to be yukking it up, there may be room for a well-crafted zinger. Since this kind of humor is often a tension reliever, it can seem entirely natural, even in grim situations.

Think of the Sean Connery Bond. First you have the five-minute action sequence of desperate hand-to-hand combat. Then, after Bond has electrocuted the baddie in the bathtub, he remarks, "Shocking."

And everyone laughs at the black humor, which gives the audience a chance to relax after all the tenseness. Your reader may appreciate a similar release planted at the right moment.

Here's a variation on one I put in the Ben Kincaid universe at a particularly dire moment:

> Ben: Times like this I wish I'd listened to what my mother told me when I was a boy.
> Mike: What did she tell you?
> Ben: I don't know. I didn't listen.

Well, I thought it was funny. Which suggests another of the problems with humor. There has never been any joke in the history of humanity that made everyone laugh.

Sarcasm. Sarcasm is a form of humor often employed in real life, particularly by snarky children (or perhaps it just seems that way to me) so no one should be surprised when it turns up in a novel. Is there a character in your book that could employ this particular form of wit? In the Kincaid novels, Christina makes the sarcastic remarks, usually gently commenting on Ben's many foibles. In *Shine*, all the lead characters are teenage girls, so I had many opportunities, but generally found it more fun to let Dream, the more sophisticated fashion-conscious girl, employ the sarcasm.

Sarcasm is irony plus bite. An ironic inversion of expectation coupled with a comment on the person to whom the comment is directed. Which is a complicated way of explaining something you probably already understood instinctively.

> Ben: I'm not sure I understood what Judge Derek was suggesting.
> Christina: What? With your astounding understanding of human nature?

You get the idea.

Comic Comparison. Trying to analyze the roots of humor is a fool's game because so much of what makes us laugh defies explanation. Why is it funny when Laurel and Hardy's piano rolls down the endless stairway for the fourth time? Why do we guffaw when the Three Stooges jab one another in the eyes? (Okay, maybe that's just me.) Who knows? But there are a few tried and true techniques for injecting wit into dialogue. One is to compare two unlike things for comic effect.

> Ben (carrying the bowl he found in the kitchen and eating from it): It's pretty filling, but I think there's something wrong with your trail mix.
> Christina: That's dog food.
> Ben: Ohhhh...

Or perhaps:

> Ben: I think Judge Derek is starting to like me. Did you see the way he smiled at me during my closing?
> Christina: My dog does that sometimes. It doesn't mean he's going to rule in my favor.

Comic Contrast. As you might have guessed, comic contrast is the opposite of comic comparison. You're still comparing two dissimilar things, but for the purpose of showing how they differ in a risible way.

> Aura: Yeah, I'm crazy about Dr. Coutant. She's like the mother I never knew. Except without the maternal instincts. Or the warmth. Or anything remotely motherly.

Double Meanings. You're lucky to be writing in the English language, one replete with words that have multiple meanings or similar spellings, homonyms, homophones, homographs, etc. These have the potential for confusion and thus humor. You're all familiar with the pun (sometimes understandably called "the lowest form of wit"). Still, in a pinch, who hasn't chuckled over a good one?

Usually bigger and better chuckles come from turns of phrases that become ambiguous and therefore capable of multiple interpretation, or even salacious interpretation. Much of the humor on television shows like *How I Met Your Mother* stems from the vast amount of sexual double entendre in the language—that is, ordinary words that acquire sexual meanings, perhaps because our language and its speakers never seen to tire of talking about sex.

> Guy: I'd like to see more of you in the future.
> Girl: You're saying you want me to take my clothes off?

If you've ever listened to the classic George Burns/Gracie Allen routines, you know that most of the humor stems from Gracie's supposedly ditzy misunderstanding of what people say, or Gracie taking literally what was meant figuratively.

> George: Gracie, those are beautiful flowers. Where did they come from?
> Gracie: Don't you remember, George? You said that if I went to visit Clara Bagley in the hospital I should be sure to take her flowers. So, when she wasn't looking, I did.

And of course, almost all the most memorable lines from the comedy genius Groucho Marx revolve around ambiguities and double meanings.

> Groucho: Last night I shot an elephant in my pajamas. How that elephant got in my pajamas I'll never know.

> Groucho: Outside of a dog, a book is man's best friend. Inside of a dog, it's hard to read.

Sadly, Groucho wouldn't live to see how backlit book readers would spoil a great joke.

And sometimes, even the lowly play on words can be memorable. At least in my imagination:

> Stagehand: Hey, Ben, were you able to repair the light fixture?
> Ben: With assistance. Many hands make lights work.

Turning clichés and familiar axioms upside down is a field of humor unto itself. It requires people to know the cliché you're messing with, but if they do, you're likely to get the smile.

> Ben: Marcia's sleeping? In the middle of the day?
> Dave: She never met a medication she didn't like.

> Mike: Are you sure he's the one?
> Bobby: Yeah. I never forget a flake.

Pushing Your Character's Buttons

Sometimes the most riveting dialogue occurs when one character deliberately or inadvertently pushes another's emotional buttons. It's not that hard to do. We all have sensitive spots, vulnerabilities, and unresolved issues that a speaker can trip upon and a writer can exploit.

Dialogue targeting emotionally sensitive spots makes for engaging reading.

This sort of dialogue works well because when you push your character's buttons, when you set off those emotional fireworks, it's likely to generate a strong reaction, be it surprise, illumination, or even catharsis. The words fly out of a character's mouth, because they're angry, or hurt, or malicious, and the reaction those words produce will convey emotional intensity to your narrative.

Focus on the speaker's purpose when you write this kind of dialogue. Why are they saying these things? Is the point to make someone mad, to get revenge, to manipulate, to confuse, to flatter, to seduce, to dazzle—or something else entirely? If you understand your character's motivation, what they hope to accomplish, it will be much easier to write interesting dialogue for them.

Next time you look at a list of classic movie lines, note how many of them are push-button dialogue of this sort, words designed to produce a specific impact on the person to whom they are spoken.

Frankly, my dear, I don't give a damn. (*Gone With the Wind*)

They call me *Mister* Tibbs! (*In the Heat of the Night*)

I'm as mad as hell, and I'm not going to take this anymore! (*Network*)

Louis, I think this is the beginning of a beautiful friendship. (*Casablanca*)

You're not too smart, are you? I like that in a man. (*Body Heat*)

Finding the Better Light

You've probably heard this joke. Guy is walking down the street and beneath the corner light he sees a man on all fours staring at the pavement:

Guy: What are you doing?
Man: Looking for my contact lens.
Guy: Where did you lose it?
Man: In the alley.
Guy: If you lost it in the alley, why are you looking for it here?

Man: The light's better.

Much dialogue is written for the purpose of casting light on someone or something that's going to be important now or later in the book. This focuses the reader's attention and ideally stimulates curiosity, suspense, or anticipation. Sometimes this is as simple as directing the reader's attention to the next big plot development. "Did you see something move out there?" Other times, the dialogue can be more elegant and can create a more dramatic reader response.

The best dialogue illuminates and draws into focus some important aspect of character or plot.

Let me give you some examples.

Exaggeration/Understatement. Although exaggeration and understatement would seem to be opposites, they accomplish the same thing: focusing attention. If someone overstates the magnitude of something, the reader understands that, at least in the character's mind, it's a big deal. Ironically, understating the magnitude of something can have the same effect.

Christina: Do you think the DA is a good lawyer?
Ben: I think he's the freaking Prince of Darkness.

Or:

Jones: We can't make payroll, Boss. Again.
Ben: Are you saying we have a little debt?
Jones: I'm saying we have debt the size of Pennsylvania.

Or, on the other hand...

93

As the smoke cleared, Aura saw a platoon of armed soldiers blocking their path.

Aura: This could slow us down a bit...

The previously discussed dashes and ellipses can also be used to shed light on a subject. When one character interrupts another, or abruptly changes the subject, it suggests there's something pressing on their mind, something they can't hold back any longer. Trailing off at the end of the sentence can suggest the avoidance of a subject, which only focuses the reader's attention more intently on what the character isn't saying.

Simile/Metaphor. Most writers only turn to figurative language when they're writing narrative prose (or poetry) and that's a shame. Similes and metaphors in descriptive passages too often stand out like words waving a red flag emblazoned with: *Here's the author being clever!* When it's in dialogue, however, so long as it's true to the voice of a character with the brains and imagination to say such a thing, it can be less intrusive and more effective. And it still shows people how clever the writer is, except perhaps without waving the needy red flag begging for attention.

Figurative language, such as similes and metaphors, can create memorable dialogue.

Remember *Butch Cassidy and the Sundance Kid,* written by the brilliant William Goldman? Best dialogue metaphor of all time:

Sundance: You just keep thinking, Butch. That's what you're good at.

Butch: Boy, I got vision, and the rest of the world wears bifocals.

Brilliant and ironic, since the rapidly changing world is about to leave these two boys far behind. Here's one from my work:

Ben: You're saying they're not communicating with one another?
Christina: I'm saying it's the Tower of Babel in there.

Parallelism

Even though you want your dialogue to sound natural, there are times when it might benefit from a little overt art, not for the purpose of showing how ingenious you are but to allow the character to shine, to motivate, or to have a powerful dramatic effect. Everyone remembers the fabulous St. Crispin's Day speech in *Henry V* ("...we few, we happy few, we band of brothers..."), but lesser rhetorical flourishes have brought other scenes to life or carried powerful dramatic punches.

Employing parallelism to create syntactic symmetry or cadence can result in stirring or inspirational dialogue.

Parallelism often refers to the skill of making the individual parts of a sentence or paragraph match one another, but here I'm using it to suggest a way of putting rhythm into your dialogue. Natural speech has a rhythm, but trying to reproduce that on the page, when different people may read it differently, can be challenging. Public speakers often employ rhythmic language, or cadence, because it has an engaging quality, much like the "hook" chorus in a popular song. The repetition becomes infectious and lends power to the message.

How many memorable speeches employ some kind of repeated speech pattern? "Ask not what your country can do for you, ask what you can do for your country." Or in an earlier era, recall Lincoln referring to a government "of the people, by the people, and for the people."

Here's another passage from JFK's famous inaugural address:

> The torch has been passed to a new generation of Americans, born in this century, tempered by war, disciplined by a hard and bitter peace, proud of our ancient heritage.

This passage probably works better when a terrific orator is orating then when it's written on the printed page. On the other hand, when I'm writing Ben's closing arguments, I'm always looking for some snazzy turn of phrase or rhetorical device to remind the reader that Ben is extremely good at what he does. In my novel *The Florentine Poet*, a key plot point is Pietro's stirring speech to the people trapped in the burning stadium. I worked for days trying to come up with a speech I thought powerful—and poetic— enough to save the day.

The passage from JFK's inaugural speech has syntactic symmetry. In one clause after another, a verb (or in one case, an adjective) is followed by a memorable prepositional phrase. This creates a cadence that makes the passage memorable.

Who can forget the stirring words Churchill used to bolster the spirits of his island nation as they prepared to go to war against a far better armed and more aggressive enemy?

> [W]e shall not flag or fail. We shall go on to the end. We shall fight in France, we shall fight on the seas and oceans, we shall fight with growing confidence and growing strength in the air, we shall defend our island, whatever the cost may be. We shall fight on the beaches, we shall fight on the landing grounds, we shall fight in the fields and in the streets, we shall fight in the hills; we shall never surrender...

Normally, you wouldn't want to start one sentence after another with the same word or words, but here it's acceptable because the reader knows it's being done deliberately for rhetorical impact. And it might well be more natural for most characters to say "will" than "shall," but in this circumstance, "shall" gives it extra oomph, as if Churchill is suggesting an affirmative duty rather than a mere prediction. Without question, there is cadence in this passage, even though the length of the sentences varies somewhat, culminating in the powerful averment that "we shall never surrender." Parliament rose to its feet in thunderous applause and cheering when Churchill finished this speech. Can you see why?

The opportunity to write dialogue of this nature will likely occur at best once per book. Make sure that when the time comes, you make the most of it.

Paying It Forward

One of the best reasons for outlining, planning ahead, and thinking about your book before your write it (see my book on Structure) is that it gives you opportunities to plant bits of business early in the book that will pay off later. This is the sort of device you are unlikely to stumble across by accident. Maybe you can inject it somewhere during the editing and revision process, but in all likelihood, either you plan it in advance or it isn't going to happen. One of the best places to plant these seeds is dialogue.

Dialogue planted to setup and payoff later can provide powerful moments of resolution, closure, and emotional resonance.

In terms of plot, a setup occurs when something happens early in the book that may seem unimportant or insignificant at the time but turns out to have enormous importance in the climax, or emotional significance in the denouement.

One of the most memorable examples of this in our modern era comes from the classic *Casablanca*. Richard Blaine (Bogey) initially introduces "Here's looking at you, kid" as a toast during a romantic moment when the two former lovers are about to love again. But at the end of the picture, as Blaine makes the noble sacrifice, sending the woman he loves off with the freedom fighter who needs her by his side, he uses the line to say goodbye, and without expressly stating it, to tell her that he still loves her.

In my book *The Midnight Before Christmas*, my protagonist Megan McGee feels lonely and alone at Christmastime, as so many do. She's recently lost her mother (in the Oklahoma City bombing) and has no one in her life but a disagreeable dog. But at the end of the book, as a result of the dramatic events in the denouement (which I am not going to spoil here), she realizes how foolish she's been. "I'm not alone. I was never alone." Many readers have told me this passage brought them courage and warmth during a difficult holiday season. It only packs that punch because it refers back to Megan's despondent ruminations earlier in the book.

In another of my books, the young adult novel *The Black Sentry*, Daman Adkins is the protagonist in a story set in a dystopian future. Daman fears his Winnowing, the armed combat all boys are required to undergo on their sixteenth birthday that determines the course of the rest of their life. He escapes his formal Winnowing, but in the climactic scene, undergoes a far more harrowing test. When he triumphs, he realizes that his earlier failures were not due to any weakness on his part but because he didn't believe in the cause for which he was fighting—until now. "I won my real Winnowing," he says. "The one that matters."

This exchange between setup and payoff can be one of the most powerful elements of a good novel. Think about the emotional core of your character—what does he or she want or need most? Can you give it to them at the end, perhaps in an unexpected way but one that is ultimately more meaningful? And can you use dialogue to highlight what has happened, to shed illumination upon it, without spelling it out so explicitly as to undercut its power?

Highlights

1) The best dialogue has emotional impact.

2) Humorous dialogue enlivens almost any scene.

3) Dialogue targeting emotionally sensitive spots makes for engaging reading.

4) The best dialogue illuminates and draws into focus some important aspect of character or plot.

5) Figurative language, such as similes and metaphors, can create memorable dialogue.

6) Employing parallelism to create syntactic symmetry or cadence can result in stirring or inspirational dialogue.

7) Dialogue planted to setup or payoff can provide powerful moments of resolution, closure, and emotional resonance.

Red Sneaker Exercises

1) Some writers can write funny and some can't. Even some people who are quite funny in real life don't write that way. And sadly, there are few things more painful to read than attempts at humor that fall flat. Which are you? Try creating a witty character that can spout witty remarks at appropriate times. Do they improve your scene?

2) Try rewriting a scene to enrich the subtext. In the first draft, you probably had the characters exchange whatever information needed to be exchanged to advance the plot. Now see if you can eliminate some of that overt telling and create a sense of "there's something that's not being said?"

3) If your dialogue seems dull or rambling, first consider shortening it, and then consider adding some remark or jab that cuts to the quick of the other character's emotional vulnerabilities. What's the point of making such a remark? What impact does it have on the person who hears it?

4) Does one of your characters have a moment when they need to deliver a stirring oration, peroration, or call to battle? If so, try using parallelism and syntactic symmetry to create a more memorable rhetorical argument or emotional high.

5) Is there something that happens near the start of your book that can be paid off at the end? If not, can you add something? Examine what you have in your denouement. Will it make your reader laugh, or cry, or feel that this has been a rewarding and worthwhile reading experience? And if not, consider the possibility of using setup and payoff to create a more satisfying and emotional moment.

6) Nothing is more challenging than trying to come up with an original piece of figurative language, something that will zero in on exactly what you're trying to say without drawing too much attention to itself. Consider reading

some of your favorite poets and examining how they employed simile, metaphor, personification, or sonic devices such as alliteration and consonance. Does that help you create a memorable and incisive phrase?

APPENDIX A: DIALOGUE CHECKLIST

Here's a shortlist of the characteristics of dynamic, memorable dialogue, followed by a list of the faults most commonly found in poor dialogue.

Great Dialogue...

Imparts a sense of realism (without necessarily being realistic)

Reveals character

Advances the story

Suggests what is not being said

Reveals hidden motivations

Reflects the characters' history (or perhaps baggage)

Reflects the hierarchal relationship between the person speaking and the person or persons listening

Refers back to something said earlier

Foreshadows what is yet to come

Has a purpose

Has emotional impact

Is memorable or even quotable

And poor dialogue…

Sounds artificial, stiff, or wooden

Seems stilted or unnatural

Contains too much exposition

Is too on-the-nose

Only conveys the obvious, or what the reader already knows

Has all the characters sounding alike

Has characters calling each other by name too often

Has too many conversational stutters, slang terms, colloquialisms, or pointless chitchat

Conveys dialect or foreign languages phonetically

Contains unnecessary attributions

DYNAMIC DIALOGUE

Uses attributions or stage directions to convey emotional information that should be imbedded in the dialogue itself

Is riddled with exclamation points

Is riddled with profanity

Uses synonyms and substitutes for "said" to no good purpose

Is dull circular, or monotonous

APPENDIX B: SUBTEXT

In the most powerful dialogue, what is unspoken is as important or perhaps even more important than what is spoken. Here are some suggestions for subtexts that could be embedded in your scenes for the reader to discern by reading between the lines.

Baggage from a personal relationship

The hunger for acceptance or affection

Secret longing or love

Bitterness or resentment

Malicious intent

Sexual predation

Envy

Social climbing aspirations

Competitiveness

Sibling rivalry

WILLIAM BERNHARDT

Parental inadequacy

APPENDIX C: DIALOGUE REVISION

Here are some guidelines for revising your dialogue:

Reread the dialogue by itself.
- Does it sound conversational?
- Are contractions, run-on sentences, and fragments used naturally?
- Does the conversational style match the mood or personality of the character?
- Does the conversational style match the dramatic or emotional intensity of the scene?
- How often do characters call each other by name? (Keep this to a minimum)
- Is there too much infodumping or exposition?

Double-check mechanics.
- Did you start a new paragraph for each new speaker? (Don't forget to indent)
- Is the punctuation inside the quotation marks?
- Did you use ellipses for pauses and trailing off, but double dashes (aka "em-dashes") for interrupted dialogue?
- Did you go easy on the exclamation marks?

Scrutinize your dialogue tags.

- Have you cut most tags other than "said?"
- Did you cut as many adverbs as possible from your tags?
- Have you cut or edited awkward or redundant speaker attributions?
- Can you cut some speaker attributions altogether?

Consider your beats.

- How many beats do you have? How often do you interrupt your dialogue? (It may be useful to highlight all your beats. Do you have too many?)
- Are you too repetitive with your beats? (For instance, do your characters sigh, blush, and raise their eyebrows a little too often?)
- Do your beats help illuminate your characters? Are they individualized or just generic, everyday actions?
- Do your beats fit the rhythm of your dialogue?

APPENDIX D: COMMONLY CONFUSED WORDS

Affect/Effect: Contrary to the commonly espoused rule, both words can be used as nouns and verbs, depending upon your meaning. *Affect* is usually a verb meaning "to have an effect on," but it can also be used to mean "countenance" or "emotion," as in, "The Vulcan had a flat affect." *Effect* is usually a noun meaning "impact" or "consequence," but it can also be used as a verb (a shortened form of "effectuate") meaning "to bring about."

Aggravate/Irritate: *Aggravate* means to worsen. *Irritate* means to inflame or anger. Many people use *aggravate* to mean "vex, annoy, or irritate," but that is not strictly speaking correct.

Allude/Refer: Yes, there is a difference. To *allude* is "to hint at or mention indirectly." To *refer* is "to mention directly." "Are you alluding to my height when you call me 'Napoleon?'" "You're short," she said, referring to his height.

Alternate/Alternative: *Alternate* means "one after the other." *Alternative* means "one instead of the other." Walking requires the *alternate* use of the left and right foot. The *alternative* is the bus.

Amused/Bemused: *Amused* means you're having a good time. *Bemused* means you're befuddled or puzzled or deep in thought.

Attorney General/Attorneys General: The plural of *attorney general* is *attorneys general*, as in: "Several assistant attorneys general appeared on behalf of the state." In this phrase, *general* is an adjective following the noun (a postpositive adjective), not a noun. The same is true of "Presidents Elect" or "mothers-in-law" or "passersby," but is not correct for a true compound word such as "spoonful." The plural would be "spoonfuls," not "spoonsful."

Besides/Beside: *Besides* means other than or in addition. *Beside* means alongside. "No one *besides* her son could stand so close beside her."

Big of a/Big of: As always, eliminate unnecessary words that add nothing to the sentence. Don't say, "How *big a* case is it?" The same is true of "long of a" "slow of a" and other similar constructions.

Childlike/Childish: *Childish* is a pejorative adjective suggesting that someone is acting like a child and that isn't good. The positive way of saying the exact same thing is *childlike*.

Complement/Compliment: To *complement* is to complete or pair with or round out. To *compliment* is to praise.

Continuous/Continual: *Continuous* means uninterrupted.

Continual means repeated, but intermittent. "Jack had to wind the grandfather clock continually to make it run continuously."

Convince/Persuade: You *convince* someone of something, but you *persuade* them to do something. *Convince* is usually followed by "that" or "of," but *persuade* is always followed by "to."

Corroborate/Collaborate: To *corroborate* evidence is to fortify it with additional evidence. To *collaborate* on a project is to work with someone else on it.

Could/Couldn't Care Less: If your intent is to say that you care as little as it is possible to care, use the phrase "couldn't care less." If you could care less, that means you already care at least a little.

Counsel/Council: *Counsel* means "advice," but it can also be a noun meaning "lawyer" or "consultant," in effect, a shortened form of "counselor." *Council* is a committee that leads or governs.

Credulous/Incredible: The *incredible* is unbelievable. Credulous people are gullible. *Incredulous* means you do not believe.

Datum/Data: *Datum* is the traditional singular, *data* the plural, but today, many people use *data* as a singular noun and few dictionaries or grammarians are still suggesting that it is incorrect.

Deserts/Desserts: In this example: What one deserves is one's *just deserts*. This use of *deserts* is related to the verb *deserve*. "The unsuccessful plaintiff got his just deserts." Deserts are dry, arid, sandy places, preferably in Cabo, and desserts include tiramisu and sopaipillas.

Discreet/Discrete: *Discreet* means "careful" or "prudent." *Discrete* means "separate, distinct, or unconnected." "Jack was *discreet* about his secret for maintaining two wives and two *discrete* households."

Disinterested/Uninterested: *Disinterested* means impartial or fair. *Uninterested* means not interested, bored, unengaged. "The judge was disinterested in the outcome of the case, and uninterested in the uncivil behavior of the divorce attorney."

Divorcé/Divorcée: *Divorcé* is for men, *divorcée* is for women.

Elicit/Illicit: To *elicit* is to evoke. *Illicit* means "illegal."

Emigrate/Immigrate: It's all about coming and going. You *emigrate* from a country and *immigrate* to another. For a mnemonic, remember that "exit" starts with an "e," like "*emigrate*," and "in" starts with an "i," like "*immigrate*."

Eminent/Imminent/Immanent: *Eminent* means "famous or superior." *Imminent* means "impending." *Immanent* (rare these days, outside of the church) means "inherent or dwelling within."

Farther/Further: *Farther* refers to physical distance. *Further* means "to a greater extent or degree."

Fewer/Less: "Fewer" is used when the items in question can be counted. "Less" is used for items not subject to easy enumeration. "We had *fewer* writers than we'd hoped for, but *less* optimism than I expected." Obviously, the sign in every supermarket reading "Ten Items or Less" is just wrong.

Hadn't/Hadn't of: "*Hadn't of*" is ugly and grammatically incorrect.

Hanged/Hung: Murderers and horse thieves used to be *hanged*. "Hung" is incorrect in that context. But paintings and coats are *hung*.

Historic/Historical: *Historic* means "having a place in history." *Historical* means "pertaining to the subject of history."

Home in/Hone in: "We need to *home* in on the precise problem."

Imply/Infer: To imply means to suggest something. To infer means to conclude from available evidence. Speakers imply. Listeners infer. Writers imply. Readers infer. "You imply that I'm a moron," the husband said. "You infer correctly," the wife replied.

Ingenuous/Ingenious: *Ingenuous* means naïve, frank, or candid, coming from the same root word as "ingénue."

Ingenious means crafty. Disingenuous means dishonest.

It's/Its: *It's* is the contraction for *it is*. *Its* is a possessive pronoun.

Jones's/Joneses: One guy is a *Jones*, but the whole family are the *Joneses*. If you are discussing something they own, that would be the *Joneses'*. The same is true of other family names ending in "s."

Laudable/Laudatory: *Laudable* means praiseworthy. *Laudatory* means praiseful. "He did a laudable job of reading the laudatory psalms."

Lie/Lay: *Lie* means to recline. The simple past tense of *lie* is *lay* and the past participle is *lain*. Lay can also be a verb indicating placement, and therein lies the confusion. The past tense of *lay* is *laid*. "Today you *lie* in the same bed where I lay my car keys."

Memoranda/Memorandum: *Memoranda* is plural, *memorandum* is singular.

Neither/Nor: Whether the verb in a "neither/nor" sentence is singular or plural depends upon the second element. Therefore, "Neither you nor I *am* responsible," but, "Neither I nor they *are* responsible." "Neither" by itself means by implication "neither one," so it takes a singular verb, as in, "Neither of your objections *is* correct." The same is true for "either," as in: "Either the plaintiff or one of the other lawyers *is* responsible for the judge's verdict."

Number/Amounts: Countable items have a *number*. Non-countable items are measured in *amounts*.

Overflowed/Overflow: *Overflowed* is the past tense and past participle of the verb *overflow*.

Persecute/Prosecute: To *persecute* is to torment. To *prosecute* is to conduct criminal proceedings. "The defendant felt *persecuted* when the DA *prosecuted* him the second time."

Principal/Principle: *Principal* means "main or primary." *Principle* means "rule or standard." "The school principal said his principal goal was to reinvest the trust fund principal, as a matter of principle."

Prophesy/Prophecy: *Prophesy* is a verb meaning "to foretell." *Prophecy* is a noun indicating what was foretold. "Madame Martel dropped her fee per prophecy, because she could prophesy a downturn in the economy."

Prospective/Perspective: *Prospective* means "potential." *Perspective* means "viewpoint."

Ravage/Ravish: A famous headline in a Minnesota newspaper read: "Queen Elizabeth Ravished." As you might have guessed, the ocean liner *Queen Elizabeth* caught fire and burned, and the paper should have said "Queen Elizabeth Ravaged" (though that sill doesn't sound very good). *Ravaged* means "damaged or destroyed." *Ravished* means "carried away (by force or by emotion) or sexually assaulted." When you say that your sweetheart looked *ravishing*, you're not implying a desire to do anything illegal. You're saying the sight of her swept you away with emotion.

Regardless/Irregardless*:* *Irregardless* is still considered substandard by most authorities, though it technically has the same meaning as "regardless."

Regretful/Regrettable: *Regretful* means "full of regret." *Regrettable* means "unfortunate, a cause for regret." "Florence *regretfully* swept up the pieces of the Ming vase she had *regrettably* smashed."

Reigned/Reined*:* "The legal fees when Queen Elizabeth reigned had to be *reined* in by the Privy Council."

Reluctant/Reticent: Although people often use these as synonyms, their true meanings aren't even similar. *Reluctant* means unwilling, but *reticent* means silent. "The *reluctant* witness was *reticent* on the witness stand."

Stationer/Stationery/Stationary*:* A *stationer* sells *stationery* (a good mnemonic device is to recall that there is an "*er*" in "*paper*"). *Stationary* objects (like stationery) do not move.

Stolen/Robbed*:* Money and other things of value are *stolen*. People, places, and businesses are *robbed*.

Therefore/Therefor*:* *Therefore* means "accordingly" or "in conclusion." *Therefor* is an ugly and archaic piece of legalese meaning "for it" or "for them," as in, "He bought a bicycle and paid *therefor*."

Tortuous/Torturous: *Tortuous* means "winding or crooked or twisty." *Torturous* means "painful." "During the tortuous drive, Jack developed a torturous ache in his backside."

Who/Whom: Most modern grammarians now say "who" can always be used in place of "whom" at the beginning of a sentence or clause. "Whom" should still be used after a preposition. So "Who from?" is correct, but so is "From whom?" Most American lexicographers, from Daniel Webster on down, have argued for clarifying the confusion by eliminating "whom" altogether, but it hasn't happened yet.

Whose/Who's: *Whose* is the possessive relative pronoun. *Who's* is the contraction for *who is*. "*Who's* the person for *whose* benefit the trust fund was established?"

APPENDIX E: COMMONLY MISSPELLED WORDS

acknowledgment*:* Most dictionaries permit *acknowledgement* but prefer to drop that extra e. Neither is incorrect.

acquiesce*:* The *-sce* ending is uncommon and confusing.

aphrodisiac*:* Derived from Aphrodite, Greek goddess of love.

appropriate*:* Almost all words beginning with *ap-* are followed by another *p*, so if you have to guess, go with *app*.

camaraderie*:* If you think of the root word comrade, you'll get it wrong. Just remember that it follows a simple consonant-vowel-consonant-vowel pattern.

Caribbean*:* While you're at it, you might as well memorize the spellings of Mediterranean, Schenectady, Mississippi, Albuquerque.

cemetery*:* Just remember "three e's."

colonel*:* When my daughter was young and we played Clue, she always called my character "Colonial Mustard." Adorable, but incorrect.

commitment*:* If the suffix begins with a consonant, such as *-ment*, you do not double the previous letter.

committed: When you add *-ed* to a verb ending in a consonant, you double the consonant: *referred*.

congratulate: Sounds like that first *t* should be a *d*. You can see the word *gratis* in the middle, derived from the Latin for "gift."

conscience: This word is easy to confuse with *conscious,* even though one is a noun and the other is an adjective.

definitely: Remember that the word *finite* in the middle. So don't drop the terminal "e."

diaphragm: The *g* is silent in medical words such as *phlegm*.

dilemma: People persist in misspelling this word with an "n" in place of the second "m," and I have no idea why.

embarrass: I have to think it through every time I type this word. Two r's and two s's.

flier: The correct spelling for both the aviator and the leaflet.

forty: No "u." Not in this country.

gauge: Also *gouge*.

handkerchief: Remember that you're describing a small kerchief, one you can hold in your hand.

hemorrhage: Similar to *hemorrhoid*. Hoping neither appear in your writing.

hors d'oeuvres: I don't think even the French understand why this is spelled this way, but it is.

inoculate: You may be tempted to add another *n or another c*.

Derives from "in the eye" because *oculus* is Latin for "eye."

judgment*:* Most dictionaries now permit this spelling, but purists (and courts) tend to prefer *judgement*.

liaison*:* Any word with three consecutive vowels is bound to confuse.

lieutenant*:* Recall that the word is derived from the French word *lieu* or "place," as in "in lieu of flowers." A lieutenant is a placeholder.

limousine*:* Easy to misspell.

millennium*:* Misspelled a thousand times. The Latin word for year is *annum,* as in *per annum* or *anniversary,* which is why it is spelled with a double *n*.

misspell*:* Don't get this one wrong when you're correcting other people's spelling.

neighbor*:* I learned this in fourth grade: *i* before *e,* except after c, and when pronounced like *-ay,* as in *neighbor* and *weigh*. And there are a few other exceptions. See *weird*.

occurrence*:* See rule under *committed*.

paramour*:* You say to your sweetheart, "Oh, you!" Hence, *o-u*.

perseverance*:* A good severance package helps you persevere. And if you put the words together...

playwright*:* Wright means "maker," as in cartwright or wheelwright or wainwright or boatwright.

premiere: This refers to an event held for the first time, but if you mean a head of state or the first among many, lop off that final *e*.

questionnaire: See rule under *committed*.

receive: Classic *i* before *e* except after c.

reconnaissance: You can see at a glance why it is frequently misspelled.

reconnoiter: You can see why the military frequently shorten this to *recon*.

renaissance: Can be used without the initial capital letter to mean "rebirth."

rendezvous: More trouble from the French.

rhythm: You just have to memorize it. Same for "rhyme."

sabotage: A sabot was a wooden shoe that could be used to subvert work. Wisdom gained from *Star Trek VI: The Undiscovered Country*.

seize: Seize is an –ei word. Siege is an –ie word, although they have similar meanings.

sergeant: The military apparently have their own spelling rules.

suede: Because it derives from the French word for Swede.

supersede: If you think about the meaning, the spelling becomes more clear.

threshold: Sounds as if it should have two h's. But it doesn't.

travelling: Most dictionaries now permit it to be spelled with one or two l's. But most readers think it looks more natural with two.

weird: Following the rule we all learned in school, it should be spelled –ie. But it is, after all, weird.

APPENDIX F: THE WRITER'S READING LIST

The Chicago Manual of Style. 16th ed. Chicago: University of Chicago Press, 2010.

Cook, Vivian. *All in a Word: 100 Delightful Excursions into the Uses and Abuses of Words.* Brooklyn: Melville House, 2010.

Fowler, H.W. *Fowler's Modern English Usage.* 3rd ed. Rev. Ernest Gowers. N.Y. & Oxford: Oxford University Press, 2004.

Goldman, William. *Adventures in the Screen Trade: A Personal View of Hollywood and Screenwriting.* New York: Grand Central, 1989.

Hale, Constance. *Sin and Syntax: How to Create Wickedly Effective Prose.* New York: Broadway Books, 2001.

Hart, Jack. *A Writer's Coach: The Complete Guide to Writing Strategies That Work.* New York: Anchor Books, 2006.

Jones, Catherine Ann. *The Way of Story: The Craft and Soul of Writing.* Studio City: Michael Wiese Productions, 2007.

Klauser, Henriette Anne. *Writing on Both Sides of the Brain*. San Francisco: Harper & Row, 1987.

Maass, Donald. *The Fire in Fiction: Passion, Purpose, and Techniques to Make Your Novel Great*. Cincinnati: Writers Digest Books, 2009.

Maass, Donald. *Writing the Breakout Novel: Insider Advice for Taking Your Fiction to the Next Level*. Cincinnati: Writers Digest Books, 2001.

Maass, Donald. *Writing 21st Century Fiction: High Impact Techniques for Exceptional Storytelling*. Cincinnati: Writers Digest Books, 2012.

O'Conner, Patricia T. *Woe Is I: The Grammarphobe's Guide to Better English in Plain English*. 2nd ed. New York: Riverhead Books, 2003.

O'Conner, Patricia T. *Origins of the Specious: Myths and Misconceptions of the English Language*. New York: Random House, 2009.

Strunk, William, Jr., and White, E.B. *The Elements of Style*. 4th ed. N.Y.: Macmillan, 2000.

Truss, Lynne. *Eats Shoots & Leaves: The Zero Tolerance Guide to Punctuation*. New York: Gotham Books, 2005.

Vogler, Christopher. *The Writer's Journey: Mythic Structure for Storytellers and Screenwriters*. Studio City: Michael Wiese Productions, 1992.

Zinsler, William. *On Writing Well: The Classic Guide to Writing Nonfiction.* 30th Anniv. Ed. New York: Harper Perennial, 2006.

About the Author

William Bernhardt is the bestselling author of more than thirty books, including the blockbuster Ben Kincaid series of novels. In addition, Bernhardt founded the Red Sneaker Writing Center in 2005, hosting writing workshops and small-group seminars and becoming one of the most in-demand writing instructors in the nation. His programs have educated many authors now published at major New York houses. He holds a Masters Degree in English Literature and is the only writer to have received the Southern Writers Guild's Gold Medal Award, the Royden B. Davis Distinguished Author Award (University of Pennsylvania) and the H. Louise Cobb Distinguished Author Award (Oklahoma State), which is given "in recognition of an outstanding body of work that has profoundly influenced the way in which we understand ourselves and American society at large." In addition to the novels, he has written plays, including a musical (book and music), humor, nonfiction books, children's books, biography, poetry, and crossword puzzles. He is a member of the Author's Guild, PEN International and the American Academy of Poets.